What Fish Don't Want You to Know

What Fish Don't Want You to Know

An Insider's Guide to Freshwater Fishing

FRANK P. BARON

Ragged Mountain Press / McGraw-Hill

Camden, Maine • New York • Chicago • San Francisco • Lisbon • London • Madrid • Mexico City • Milan • New Delhi • San Juan • Seoul • Singapore • Sydney • Toronto

The McGraw·Hill Companies

1 2 3 4 5 6 7 8 9 0 DOC DOC 0 10 9 8 7 6 5 4 3

Library of Congress Cataloging-in-Publication Data
Baron, Frank P.
  What fish don't want you to know : an insider's guide to freshwater fishing / Frank P. Baron.
        p.   cm.
Includes index.
  ISBN 0-07-141714-1
  1. Fishing. 2. Freshwater fishes. I. Title.
  SH441.B325 2003
  799.1´1—dc21   2003010533

Questions regarding the content of this book should be addressed to
Ragged Mountain Press
P.O. Box 220
Camden, ME 04843
www.raggedmountainpress.com

Questions regarding the ordering of this book should be addressed to
The McGraw-Hill Companies
Customer Service Department
P.O. Box 547
Blacklick, OH 43004
Retail customers: 1-800-262-4729
Bookstores: 1-800-722-4726

Photo on pages ii–iii and vi–vii by Peter Essick/AURORA. Photo of lure on chapter openers by Keith Walters. All other photographs by the author unless otherwise indicated.
Illustrations by Jonathan Milo.

For Dad, who took me fishing and taught me that these finned critters were worthy of respect, and yes, love. And for Mom, who, with patience and humor, raised a family of anglers.

CONTENTS

PREFACE

A fisherman is a jerk at one end of a line, waiting for a jerk at the other.

—Anonymous

This book is about catching freshwater fish—mostly trout, walleye, salmon, bass, muskie, and pike—using standard, open-faced spinning gear. If you use a spincast outfit or level wind-casting reel, don't worry, most of the information here is applicable. (If you're *really* new to this fishing thing and are scratching your head right now, you should check out the primer on page 153.)

I'm tempted to say that everyone on the planet would benefit from reading this book, but that would be a lie. And, as everyone well knows, fishermen never lie.

The truth is, my target reader is the neophyte angler (but one who knows which end of the rod to hold), the angler who fishes several times a year, and the hard-core, advanced angler.

Beginners will find a valuable condensed library of information at their fingertips.

Occasional anglers will learn some new techniques and refinements that will improve their catching consistency.

And advanced anglers will enjoy the huge ego boost of flipping through the pages while muttering, "I knew that."

I will reluctantly admit that there are a few anglers who won't get much out of these pages. Fly fishermen, for example, will learn no new techniques, although they might learn something useful about their target fish's habits and habitat.

And save your money if you are among the breed of anglers I call "fishin' technicians." These folks are instantly recognizable, as they rarely actually *fish*. They spend most of their time cruising the water at just below warp-speed, eyes glued to a mesmerizing array of blinking LEDs and LCDs on their sonars, temperature probes, oxygen and pH meters, GPS, and underwater cameras.

They are often just too darn busy to get around to tossing out a line.

I'm not antitechnology. I approve of, and use, some of these tools in the same way I do alcohol—in moderation. But you are holding the wrong book if you're looking for a lot of high-tech information.

My fisherman, the one I wrote this book for, is one whose mind and senses are focused on solving the mystery of what happens when the line disappears into the water.

I am well aware, and pleased, that a significant and growing percentage of anglers are women. But I really hate carefully constructed, politically correct, gender-neutral language. For that reason, I don't use the term "fisherperson" in this book. Nor does the oft-used "fisher" appear. A fisher is a small mammal related to the weasel. It may be adept at catching fish, but I have never seen one with a rod in its paws.

I most often use the word "angler," an acceptable gender-neutral term, but I also use "fisherman" with some degree of regularity. In my personal lexicon, it is an umbrella word that encompasses both sexes.

The word "Other," with a capital "O," also appears from time to time. I use it to denote all those unfortunates who not only do not fish but who are bewildered or even aghast at those of us who do.

Most Others are characterized by their total inability to understand that standing for hours in thigh-deep, freezing water during a sleet storm, while catching nothing but frostbite, is a heck of a lot of fun. These Others, usually our spouses, acquaintances, and coworkers, should be treated with kindness. Their lack of understanding is based on ignorance, and they are more to be pitied than scorned.

Some Others, unfortunately, have mutated into "Antis." Their benign condescension somehow turned to disdain and antipathy. They do not like what we do and want us to stop. The Antis are to be ignored at our peril. I address their concerns in chapter 8, Etiquette and Ethics.

Some parts of this book are highlighted. Just like in school, these are the most important bits of information, and the test will come on the water. Some of these highlighted areas are "rules." Very, very few of them are absolute. In some instances, I'll mention the exceptions; in most, I won't. Part of the fun of fishing is finding them on your own.

When the idea of writing a book about fishing first occurred to me, I thought it would be a quiet, meditative reflection on the spiritual aspects of my beloved pastime.

Didn't happen.

While a few contemplative thoughts crept in, I found I could not ignore the fact that fishing is just plain fun. And, so, my "hymn of praise" evolved into a "how-to with humor."

I had fun writing it. I hope you have fun reading it.

Shall I go to heaven or a-fishing?
—Henry David Thoreau

ACKNOWLEDGMENTS

Since this book encompasses about 45 years of experience, the list of people who have contributed is lengthy. Most shall remain nameless, but they include everyone with whom I've fished, mentors, and peers.

I am very grateful for the support and encouragement of my family and friends, especially my brother Karl, for proofing my first draft and providing pictures. Thanks also to Evan Linnell (www.magicportraits.net) and Justin Hoffman (www.geocities.com/natureseyeimages/stockpage.html) for their photos.

I am beholden to Mr. Ernest H. Winter, my high school English teacher, for convincing me I was a talented writer and for not looking kindly at work that was less than my best.

During the actual writing process, my online community of friends contributed invaluable encouragement, comments, and advice. Thank you Pam, Lu, Abby, and Cay. Thanks to my friends at #WritingWest.

And a tip of the hat to My Kindly Editor, Tristram Coburn. Tris took a chance on an unknown Canadian writer-angler and hoodwinked his bosses into publishing him. Along this sometimes-bumpy road he was a calm touchstone, unfailingly positive and reassuring.

I would also be remiss if I didn't thank every one of the many thousands of fish that made my rod bend, my heart race, and my spirit soar.

Very young author (left) proudly shows off a small-mouth bass.

In the Beginning

When I was very young, fishing was something my father and his friends did that involved getting up before dawn, coming home after dark, and smelling funny. Upon his return, Dad would proudly open his willow creel, and I would peer in, fascinated by the plump, shiny, brightly colored fish. He told me that these were trout, usually browns or brookies, and sometimes rainbows.

I liked the look of those fish. I liked the smell. I liked the satisfied tiredness I read in my dad's smile. By the time I was six, he had a hard time sneaking off without me.

The sportscasters at ABC's *Wide World of Sports* probably believe they redefined the phrase "the agony and the ecstasy."

Wrong.

The agony and the ecstasy is a six-year-old boy trying to go to sleep, knowing he's going fishing in the morning. It's trying to nod off fully clothed, except for the rubber boots beside the bed. It's being tormented by the despairing certainty that the trout will be feeding ravenously and that we'll run out of worms. It is the dreadful fear that I will fail to rouse when my father calls and that he'll leave without me. It's wondering if my rod and line will be strong enough if I hook The-Biggest-Trout-In-The-Whole-Stream.

The night's torments are a distant memory as we creep down the stairs in the dark. Anticipation blossoms and swells as we whisper in the kitchen. The magic of being awake as my mother, brothers, and sisters (and the rest of the world) remain asleep is intoxicating. I smell the coffee, gulp my cereal, and pepper my father with dozens of questions as he makes our sandwiches. Where are we going? How long does it take to get there? Do we have enough

NOT-SO-TALL TALES

Wherever and whenever anglers gather, stories are told. I loved listening to my father, my uncles, and their friends when they got together to swap yarns. The passage of time, and a forever-evolving Heightened Awareness (more on that later), resulted in tales of fish of staggeringly gargantuan proportions.

I've spent enough time on the water now to have a few of my own tales to tell. Often, my favorite memories aren't of the biggest fish or of days when I caught the most fish. Instead, those memories concern fish that for reasons of time or circumstance stand out in my mind like they were caught this morning. You'll find these Not-So-Tall Tales throughout this book. I hope you enjoy them. ◄◄

worms? What kind of trout are there? Which one do you think is the biggest? Are you sure we have enough worms?

I remember sitting in the backseat, content to listen as Dad and his friends discussed the day to come. I filed away tidbits of information: sometimes half a worm is best . . . look for the holes under the bank . . . don't use too heavy a sinker. What I *don't* recall are too many specifics about those trips.

The memories are a blur of tangled lines, too-tall ferns, chattering streams, and the occasional trout. I don't know if it happened instantly or over a period of time, but before too long the only thing I wanted to *do* was go fishing. The only thing I wanted to *be* was a good fisherman.

Back then, defining the term "good fisherman" was easy. A good fisherman was one who caught a lot of fish. Over the years, my definition has changed quite a bit, but I devoted my teens and early twenties to realizing that early one.

I read hundreds of magazine articles and wrote a few myself. I spent thousands of hours on the water. And I satisfied that early desire; I caught a *lot* of fish.

Over the years I've learned something simple, yet significant: *There are only two ways to catch a fish by angling.*

Yep, only two (that is, "2," "II").

Neither of them requires a Ph.D. You don't need to know the dissolved oxygen content at the thermocline. You don't even need to know what the thermocline *is* (but it might help, so I'll tell you later).

You don't have to have a bass boat rigged with enough electronics to power a small town. You can catch fish without using the latest rod, thinnest line, or newest never-fail lure. You don't need an awful lot of what advertisers and fishin' technicians say you need.

What you *do* need is time, patience, a little knowledge, and the angler's best friend, luck.

The time and patience are up to you.

Luck is in the lap of the gods.

The little knowledge is in this book.

CHAPTER 1

Thinking Like a Fish

One of the keys to catching fish is knowing how they think. "Thinking like a fish" has become something of a cliché, but it is essential if you want to improve your results. (By the way, it doesn't help to stare bug-eyed at the water while rhythmically gulping air. I've tried it.)

You need both *general* and *species-specific* knowledge to truly get inside their slippery little heads.

On the general level, fish aren't much different from you and me. Our most basic needs are food and shelter. When these are met, we look at a whole range of other things to occupy our time. *Fish don't.* Except at spawning time, fish are pretty much locked into the food and shelter thing.

They will find and spend most of their time in safe, comfortable places near food. To catch them, you must find these safe, comfortable places and offer them food (or a reasonable facsimile).

That's where the species-specific knowledge comes in. A sunfish's definition of "safe and comfortable" is vastly different from that of a 40-pound muskie. Even the ranking of safe and comfortable is on a sliding scale. The sunfish has many enemies and will choose safety over comfort if it can't have both. The muskie fears little and will take comfort every time.

All species want food nearby.

It's important to understand that all fish are in harmony with and finely attuned to their environments. They utilize their senses to the utmost, always aware of danger, always alert to the presence of prey. This near-constant state of high alert works against the plodding, clumsy, gravity-challenged angler. Luckily for us, though, fish aren't particularly smart, and they're *great* opportunists. That is the edge we have to exploit.

I've caught thousands of fish on live and artificial worms or grubs. Chances are, few of those fish had ever seen either one before in their natural environments. They took the bait because it smelled good and looked helpless.

▶ **This "good to eat + can't hurt me" thinking is the undoing of many a fish.**

So, in a nutshell, "thinking like a fish" means assessing a body of water, determining where your fish is likely to be, and then giving it what it thinks it wants. Let's look at some typical bodies of water to see how this works.

Small Streams

I cut my angling teeth fishing small creeks and streams for trout. Water like this is the easiest to "read" (to figure out where the fish are). Most of what follows applies to native fish, those that are born in, and that stay in, a particular body of water. Migratory trout and salmon are different and I'll cover them on page 10 and elsewhere.

Fish don't like light. They have no eyelids (can't blink) and no external ears (nowhere to hang sunglasses). They also have enemies, so they don't want to be seen. Consequently, fish avoid light. So look for them in the deeper, darker holes, brush-covered areas, under overhangs, and deep within undercut banks.

Fish are lazy. Or, if you prefer, extremely "energy efficient." They want food to come to them rather than to have to actually hunt for it. Aquatic insects, such as nymphs and larva, and unlucky terrestrials, like ants and grasshoppers, form the basis of their diet. As the insects hatch or the luckless ants lose their grip, the current tumbles them downstream. The biggest, most aggressive, "boss" fish will stake out the best holes in the stream, those that provide safety and proximity to a good current. Like a pizza place, the current offers free home delivery.

Fish seek shadowed areas to avoid being seen by predators. The shade provided by overhead cover also cools the water.

Being both lazy and cautious, they won't spend a lot of time in mid-current, but will dart out from cover to snap up a morsel and then retreat. In deep, dark holes, the depth at the mid-to-lower part of the pool provides a respite from the current, and the fish can pick and choose from the smorgasbord that comes their way.

Fish are agoraphobic (they have a fear of open spaces). You would be too if ospreys, kingfishers, gulls, and eagles had 20-foot wingspans and enjoyed eating people.

Therefore, fish want a "roof" over their heads. The roof usually takes three forms: cover (as in tree roots, undercut banks, overhanging brush, or even surface foam), depth, and turbidity. Depth offers safety if predators can't see to bottom where the fish is hunkered down. And dingy water allows fish to go about their business with less likelihood of being seen.

You will rarely, if ever, see a "boss" native fish before you've hooked it. It will be tucked away under the bank or under another obstruction if available. If you can see the bottom of a pool, the "ceiling" is too low for a good fish to feel comfortable. It will find a safer place.

In moving water such as streams and rivers, the current delivers food to fish.

You'll come across water that seems to fit the bill, deep holes with brush or overhangs, and catch nothing but chubs or suckers. What's the deal?

The water is probably moving too slowly, with either not enough oxygen or uncomfortably high temperatures and a poor delivery system. A nearby current flow is essential.

▶ **Exception: Occasionally, usually at night or after a rain, some big fish will visit these holes to put a dent in the chub and sucker population.**

OK, you're fishing a stream and you've found a likely looking hole that satisfies all the criteria. Now what?

Well, if you're a member of PETA (People for the Ethical Treatment of Animals), you take a picture and go home.

But you happen to be an angler, and you want a crack at that 16-inch brown you just *know* is in there somewhere.

Before we get too far along here, let's take a peek at what you're wearing and what tackle you're using. (I'll go into greater depth on these subjects in chapters 3 and 6.)

You have hip waders on because it will be necessary to cross the stream several times during the course of the day. Some holes can only be properly approached from one side or the other. And you'll usually want to face the sun to keep your shadow behind you.

You have a vest on with a minimum of 97 pockets, all of which are bulging with stuff you will mostly never need but that you *might* use one day. (Besides, aching shoulders are a small price to pay for a good trout.)

You are wearing a hat and polarized sunglasses to cut the glare (*facing the sun, remember?*). These items are necessary even on cloudy days. I only ditch them during a downpour.

You are using tackle suited to the conditions and your quarry. Your rod is 5 to 6½ feet long because it's a brushy creek and maneuvering a longer rod is a pain. It's a light-action rod, and your reel is spooled with 4- or 6-pound monofilament because the largest fish you are likely to encounter is 20 to 24 inches and weighs 3 or 4 pounds. The average is 8 to 14 inches. You're using a small, #10 or #12 short-shanked, wide-gapped hook (smaller than a dime) tied directly to your line. (See the primer in the appendix for hook sizes.)

You've hooked a small worm, or a piece of a large one, once through the middle. You've attached a tiny, BB shot sinker about 10 inches above your hook because the current is medium-fast.

You're ready. And you're lookin' good. Maybe someone should take *your* picture.

You take careful aim and drop your offering dead center

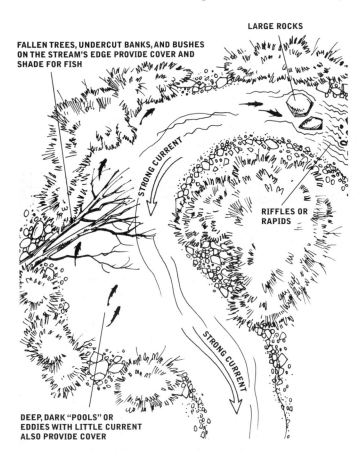

LARGE ROCKS

FALLEN TREES, UNDERCUT BANKS, AND BUSHES ON THE STREAM'S EDGE PROVIDE COVER AND SHADE FOR FISH

STRONG CURRENT

RIFFLES OR RAPIDS

STRONG CURRENT

DEEP, DARK "POOLS" OR EDDIES WITH LITTLE CURRENT ALSO PROVIDE COVER

Fish take advantage of any available cover to avoid enemies and to ambush prey. Most streams you fish will have these features: areas of strong current, riffles and rapids, runs, deep pools, rocks and boulders, and various forms of overhanging cover like bushes, fallen trees, and undercut banks.

in the middle of a nice pool with a barely perceptible *plop*. You prepare to do battle.

Wrong! Error! Stop the tape!

Remember the part about fish being finely attuned to their environment? Aha! I thought not. You just remembered the part about them being not too bright.

In the natural scheme of things, a fish doesn't often see worms dropping through its "ceiling." Their food usually drifts in gently through the "front door," via the current.

OK, roll tape.

You take careful aim and drop your offering *above* your pool, letting the current tumble your bait naturally to where Mr. 16-inch Brown is waiting, jaws agape. Tap-tap-tap, hook-set, and the battle is on!

▶ **Exception: Sometimes, especially on bright, sunny days when the water is low and clear, a fish won't come out from cover to take even the**

NOT-SO-TALL TALE

First Trout

When I caught my first trout (which *might* have been a chub or a dace—doesn't really matter, it was bright and shiny) I was probably about 5 or 6 years old. I'd memorized the description of the tap-tap feeling that meant I had a bite. I knew, in theory, how to set the hook. I was supposed to lift up the rod, hard.

I was using a push-button spincasting outfit like many youngsters start with even today. We were fishing in an open section of a small stream bordered by fields on both sides. I felt the tap-tap. I reared back on the rod. Somewhere in the process I must have put my thumb on the button when I set the hook because I recall glimpsing a small, silvery object arcing overhead and rocketing behind me to land about 25 yards away in the field. The grass and weeds in the field were as tall as I was. I remember the sunlight glinting off my line as it disappeared far into the distance. I was very excited, but felt very small.

I set my rod down and, clutching the line in my hands, traced it back into the field, hollering for Dad all the while. Together we admired the 5-inch beauty we found at the end of the line. I don't remember which of us rushed back to the creek to let it go before it died. I only remember that we did let it go. I don't recall if I caught another fish that day or not, but I'll forever remember following that shimmering line through the field. ◀◀◀

most artfully presented bait tumbling a foot or two away. If a portion of the current leads directly into the cover, let your offering go there. Hopefully, the fish will take it before you get snagged. If the fish is in an eddy near shore, try tossing your bait lightly onto the bank, and then slowly drag it until it slides into the water like an adventurous but unlucky wanderer.

Rivers

Now it gets a little trickier. The same basic rules apply to bigger moving water; fish still want to feel safe and be near food.

But they will have more choices of where to be in a larger river. Aside from the "usual" places already discussed, they may take shelter behind rocks or boulders, which provide current breaks. They will hold there sometimes, keeping their eyes focused on the sides so they can snatch passing goodies.

If you're after migratory fish, like steelhead, some browns and brookies, or salmon, you'll find them using the water as a highway to get where they are going (spawning beds) rather than as a home. They will rest in deeper holes, much to the chagrin of the natives, but won't shy away from rapids, riffles, or shallower water. (If you only got to have sex once a year, you wouldn't be bothered by trifles like food or shelter either.) These fish are also usually much larger than natives and not as worried about airborne predators.

So, unlike natives, migratory fish can be, and often are, hooked in water where they *can* be seen. You can often try to catch a specific fish, somewhat like a fly fisherman casting to where an individual fish is repeatedly rising.

I still focus on deeper holes and runs when fishing for migratory fish because I much prefer the mystery of not knowing exactly what it is that takes my offering.

You're going to look a little different when fishing these waters. You may have replaced your hip waders with chest waders so that you can negotiate deeper water. You're probably wearing the same vest, hat, and sunglasses, though.

Your rod may be anywhere from 7 to 13 feet long. The longer rods, 9-feet-plus, allow the use of light lines (4- to 8-pound test), even though your target fish may be over 20 pounds. The extra length absorbs impact, saves wear and tear on the arms, and lets you present live or artificial bait more naturally. You can keep the tip of the rod more directly above your bait, reducing line drag and making it easier to detect pick-ups.

The shorter, 7- to 9-foot rods are better for casting and retrieving hardware (spinners, plugs, and so on) and can be spooled with 8-pound or heavier line. You still present your offering, whether live or artificial, upstream from the fish, letting the current help present it.

▶ **Exception (sort of): One tactic that can work quite well, particularly with migratory fish, uses the current in a different way. Position yourself upstream of the hole and drop a wobbling-type plug into the current, holding it in place and letting the current supply the action (this is known as "back-dropping"). Every 20 seconds or so, let a little line out to ease the plug deeper into the hole. Many fish, especially big ones, find the implacable, unhurried wobbling absolutely maddening and will strike furiously. Hold on tight, because the hits are often arm-jarring.**

Ponds

Small, enclosed water, like ponds formed by beaver dams, demand the stealth of a Ninja. There are no chattering rapids to mask sound, no ripples to disguise a silhouette. Approach in a crouch, tiptoeing and taking advantage of any available cover. If there is no cover, crawl. Use light tackle and tiny lures or bait. Fish in these small, enclosed systems are acutely aware of what is "normal."

One element that can tip the scale in our favor is if the pond has a healthy population of fish. Competition can be fierce, and the first few may come easily. One day my father and I happened to be fishing a stocked pond when the hatchery truck came and off-loaded a few hundred brook (speckled) trout. We spent the next two hours catching fish with every cast. We experimented with the most unlikely baits and lures, and there was

JUSTIN HOFFMAN

Small, isolated beaver ponds require a stealthy approach and a careful presentation.

nothing those fish wouldn't hit. If it landed in the water, they raced to see who could smack it first. But about three hours later the action slowed down considerably. When I returned a couple of days later, I once again had to refine my techniques to tempt the occasional fish to bite. Even dumb-as-posts hatchery-raised fish can learn to be wary.

Float tubes are a fun alternative to canoes and boats for exploring smaller waterways.

Larger ponds often have deeper water and more cover in the form of overhangs and/or weed growth. Some ponds are big enough to explore with a canoe, jonboat, or float tube (an inner tube designed for fishing, with seats, backrests, and other amenities).

Ponds are family-friendly, and they are a great place for

introducing kids to fishing. Panfish are often plentiful and obliging, and casting accuracy isn't a prerequisite. (Perch, sunfish, rock bass, and other fish too small to be considered game fish are often referred to as panfish, and as "pan" suggests, they can be good eating!) Pack a lunch, bring along some folding chairs, and make a day of it. If the action is slow, there are birds to watch, frogs to catch, and mud to fall into.

Surprisingly large game fish may also thrive in ponds, depending on depth, oxygen content, and water temperature. Farm ponds throughout southern Canada and the U.S. host largemouth bass, some in large numbers, others with fewer but larger fish.

One of the things I love about finding a new pond is discovering what kinds of fish have made it their home. Some ponds offer a surprising array of species. I've caught brown trout of 3 pounds, and lost bigger ones, in a pond that also offers plenty of child-friendly catfish, rock bass, perch, and sunfish. Another pond I frequent once yielded eight largemouth bass between 1 and 2 pounds, four brook trout between 12 and 16 inches, two large suckers, and a 4-pound carp—all in one morning!

And, no, I am *not* going to tell you where it is!

Ponds are usually great places to introduce kids to fishing.

Dams

Dams with a good flow of water are fish magnets. They provide everything that most species of fish require: fresh oxygenated water, current flow, and shelter. Resident fish will often make dam outflows their year-round home, while migratory fish are usually slowed or stymied by dams and "stack up" below them.

Most large dams are well-known as fishing hot spots. I enjoy looking for smaller, lesser-known dams. Many ponds are dammed and have outflow areas, often beneath roads. I've driven many back roads looking for such opportunities, and I've even found a couple of working mills that utilize small ponds with flows of water below. In many instances fish can be caught both in the pond and below it at the dam outflow. (Ask for permission first if it's on private property.)

Dams with moving water are fish magnets on any watercourse. Typically, fish can be found at the lower end of the main current (1). They are also found off to the side of the more turbulent water (2) and, depending on the size of the dam, sometimes tucked behind the lip of the spillways (3).

Even many small streams have natural or beaver-engineered dams somewhere along their course. A small waterfall, even as little as 2 feet high, can carve out an attractive fish-holding pool.

Most often, fish are found waiting for their dinner at the lower end of the main current of the outflow. In deeper, more turbulent waters, they may also be off to the side in eddies where they needn't exert any excess energy while keeping an eye on the main current flow. And don't overlook the area underneath the main outflow itself. Often there is a shaded, quiet piece of underwater real estate under that arc of rushing water. Presenting a lure or bait in this area can be tricky, but it's worth the extra care and precision it may require.

The biggest fish in the area may spend its daylight hours there and come out only to forage at night or under dark, rainy conditions. But the fish probably won't ignore a juicy meal that happens to land in the vicinity while it's waiting to come out.

▶ **Dams that impede the progress of migratory fish are often declared sanctuaries and are off-limits to anglers, at least at certain times of the year. Consult your local fishing regulations.**

Lakes and Reservoirs

It can be difficult to locate fish in large bodies of water because they offer something that streams, rivers, and most ponds do not: options, and lots of them. A boss trout may occupy the same hole in a stream for years. The same fish in a lake may not be in the same area from one day to the next.

▶ **Day-to-day weather, seasonal climactic changes, and the movement of baitfish are all factors that influence where game fish hold in large bodies of water.**

The presence of food is hugely important because, unlike a stream or river, large bodies of water don't "deliver." Lake fish have to go out to eat.

I mentioned earlier that an angler needs general and species-specific knowledge, and these rules certainly apply to large bodies of water. Your target fish still want comfort, safety, and access to food.

Unlike streams and rivers, which often deliver food to fish via a current, fish in lakes and reservoirs have to go "out" to eat.

Species-specific knowledge helps to narrow the parameters. Largemouth bass usually find comfort, security, and food in different areas than walleye do, although they may share the same lake. Smallmouth bass and lake trout often inhabit the same body of water, but you'll rarely catch them back-to-back in the same spot. Many species have different temperature preferences, breeding cycles, food sources, and enemies. All these differences dictate where fish will be found in a given body of water. (See the How to Do Your Homework sidebar on page 40.)

OK, now you're standing on a dock, gazing at a large body of unfamiliar water. A hundred miles of shoreline, dozens of bays, and a sprinkling of islands present a daunting task: Where the heck are the fish?

Luckily, just as the fish have many options, so do you.

Hydrographic maps, which show lake depths and contour lines, are available for most lakes and can be invaluable. Local marinas and bait shops are often good resources for the latest scuttlebutt. They want your business and hardly ever lie.

Another advantage you have is that you can read and fish can't. You can learn their preferred habitat and forage. They don't have a clue where you live and what you like to eat.

Fish swim, rest, hide, and eat. So can you, if you want. But you can also troll, drift, cast, and still-fish. You can present lures on the surface, on the bottom, and in between.

Fish have very tiny brains. Yours is most likely *much* bigger. Fish have teeth, muscle, and fins to rely on for hunting and survival.

You have a bulging tackle box.

Fish can be buried in weeds, sheltered among boulders, cruising the surface, or suspended at 25 feet over a 70-foot bottom.

You have a bulging tackle box.

Well, you also may have a depth-finder, sometimes called a sonar unit or graph. (I dislike the term "fish-finder." These devices *cannot* be relied upon to "find" fish. They *can* be counted on to tell you where bottom is and what may be in between.)

▶ **Since most fish are on or near bottom most of the time, a depth-finder can be very helpful.**

Let's say your target species in a given body of water is walleye. From your reading and bait shop eavesdropping, you know they feed largely on

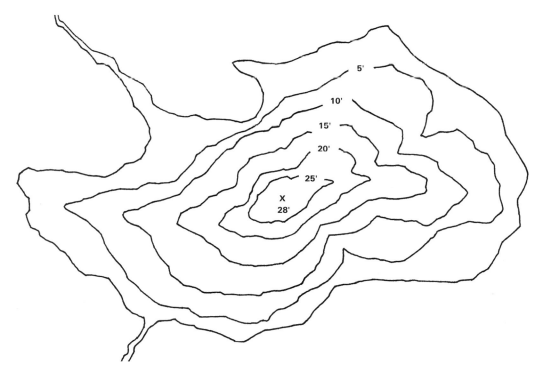

A hydrographic map, which shows lake contours and depth changes, can help pinpoint fish locations. Understanding structure and acquiring species-specific knowledge will make these maps your new best friend. Don't worry if they initially look like Greek to you—they do to everyone at first. More details to follow in the next chapter.

young perch and crayfish. Walleye are light sensitive, and the water is quite clear. Young perch are usually found around weeds, crayfish among rocks. Cloudy skies and a light chop are helping to cut the light penetration.

Your mission: find weeds and/or rocky shoals with access to deeper water (food + safety). Remember, fish are lazy; they don't want to be too far away from their munchies. After exploring for a while, you find a nice line of weeds extending from shore into about 8 feet of water. Traveling farther out, you find that the bottom drops off fairly sharply, then levels out at about 20 feet.

A school of nice-sized walleye, realizing that you are too darn smart for them, give up and start jumping into the boat . . .

Wake up!

It's never quite *that* easy.

The more you know about your target species *and* the body of water you hope to catch them in, the easier it will be to find them. Finding fish is obviously the first and most important part of catching them.

Books, magazines, television programs, government publications, and the Internet can provide solid information for your target fish. I won't slough off all responsibility, though. I *can* discuss some general information on where to find fish in large bodies of water. And that means talking about structure.

CHAPTER 2

Structure

I've read explanations of fishing structure that make quantum physics seem understandable. In a nutshell:

► **Structure is anything recognizably different from its surroundings, either above or, most often, below the surface of the water.**

A dock is structure because the water below it is darker and cooler than the surrounding water. If a shallow mud flat changes to rock and drops off to deeper water, that transition area—from mud to rock, from shallow to deeper—is structure. A rocky shoal, a clump of weeds, a point, a sunken island, a shelf, are all forms of structure.

Recognizing structure is important because fish relate to it much the way we relate to the "structures" in our lives.

Our home is the structure where we spend most of our time. It is where we feel safe and comfortable (hopefully). Fish have home bases, too. If we are too hot or too cold, we can adjust a thermostat or open or close a window. A fish, however, will alter its metabolism and, consequently, its feeding habits. Or it will move to a new home base if there is a seasonal change or if its forage moves.

If we're hungry, we can raid the fridge. Few fish have that option,

KEN GROSS

Docks offer fish shelter, shade, and a "hiding spot" from which they can ambush unwary prey. Anglers, particularly bass fishermen, should thoroughly work the water around and under docks.

although weed-oriented fish like largemouth bass, and occasionally pike and walleye, often live where they feed, sharing weeds and shallower water with panfish, minnows, and frogs.

A closer analogy to fish going off to eat is when we go out to work. We use the most efficient route to get from home to work. Often unconsciously, we use roads, signs, buildings, and landmarks to guide us, all of which are forms of structure. Fish use similar underwater structure to orient themselves when they "go to work." When our place of work changes, or if we move our home base, we need to find another route. If the fish's forage changes location, or if their home base becomes too uncomfortable, then they must change routes, too. We go where the paycheck is. They go where they can fill their bellies.

▶ **The more you learn about a game fish, its preferred temperature, its favorite forage, the easier it will be to determine the structure it will relate to. Then you have a chance to catch them where they live, where they feed, and along the route they take to get from one to the other.**

Weeds

I used to hate weeds.

Not far from my home is a shallow, weed-filled lake that hosts a large population of walleye and largemouth bass, some smallmouth, and a fair number of muskies in the 6- to 30-pound range.

I used to fish it the way everyone else did, by trolling spinners and plugs. Every minute or so, I would have to reel in and clear the hooks of weeds. It was a rare day indeed when my lure ran clear long enough to actually hook a fish.

In the late 1980s, the Erie Dearie lure caught my eye and lightened my wallet. These long, slim, jig-headed, single-blade spinners (see photo page 43) with their single hook seemed better suited to working weedy water than traditional treble-hooked lures.

Tipped with a worm and cast or trolled along—even through weeds—they worked very well. Our walleye and muskie count went up.

My usual fishing partner, my brother Karl, began dunking jig and grub combos (you can learn more about this in chapter 3) into the pockets and edges of weed as we drifted over them. This method produced very well too, and it allowed us to work weed-choked water even the Dearie couldn't plow through.

I love weeds now.

It's not uncommon for the two of us to combine for forty or so walleye a day, with a smattering of largemouth and muskies, on the same lake we used to shake our fists at.

▶ **Weeds are an important structure on any lake and should never be ignored.**

Weeds always hold minnows and smaller panfish (also known as baitfish), which often form the main diet of game fish. If the game fish aren't found right in the weeds, they usually won't be far off, at least at certain times of the year.

All weeds are not created equal, though. Some types are favored over others by certain species. One rule of thumb regarding weeds relates to color. You'll want to fish bright green weeds, indicating healthy, oxygen-producing plant growth.

Weed lines extending into deeper water usually produce better for all game fish except largemouth, which often inhabit the thickest slop in surprisingly shallow water. I also like to look for isolated weed clumps and

The shelter and oxygen weeds provide in many bodies of water attract and hold baitfish, which in turn attract and hold game fish, which in turn should attract and hold you.

The Mystery

When I was ten or eleven my father, his friend, and I spent a day fishing a creek for brown and brook trout. I seem to recall we had at least a couple of 10-inchers. Toward evening we drove to a small dam nearby. There was a pool below the dam and a pond above it. There were rumors of large browns, measured in pounds instead of inches, in the upper pond.

My father and his friend fished the pond. After a short time with them, I decided to try the pool below the dam, which was located on the outskirts of a small park, itself on the outskirts of a small village. Darkness fell, but there was enough ambient light from the park and one or two streetlights that I could see well enough to cast.

It was my first time fishing at night, and I felt proud that my father had decided I wasn't a kid anymore, as evidenced by his not hustling me home at dusk. Mixed with the pride, though, was a bit of unease. Shadows that offered friendly shade an hour before now seemed to harbor a hint of menace. The constant drumming sound of the water pouring down the dam meant I couldn't hear the voices of my father and his friend. I *knew* they were only a few yards away, up the embankment, but being unable to see or hear them spooked me a little.

All of that was forgotten a few moments later when, instead of the tap-tap I was now accustomed to, I felt a deep, insistent, throbbing thump-thump. I set the hook and my rod bent and stayed bent, but I felt life surging on the other end. No way was I snagged. I whooped and hollered and reeled and prayed, and a few minutes later I was admiring the biggest brown trout I'd ever caught. Dad heard me and clambered down to admire it. It was 16 inches long and chunky, probably close to 2 pounds. I learned that my dad's friend had caught a similar fish up above.

My father dispatched my fish, and I laid it down on the grass a few feet behind me and continued to fish. A half-hour or so of unproductive fishing followed, and I heard my dad holler that it was time to go. I reeled in and went to fetch my fish.

It was gone.

It was my first confrontation with the impossible. It had been right *there!* Yards away from the water. It was well and thoroughly dead in any case. No way did it magically transport itself back into the water. I waved for Dad and his friend, and both came down to search. No use. The fish had disappeared.

On the drive home the adults concluded that most likely I had provided an easy meal for a lucky raccoon. A cat couldn't have dragged off a fish that size without my noticing some kind of commotion.

I was crestfallen. I had *so* anticipated showing that brown off to my mother and younger brothers and sisters. Luckily, Dad backed me up, so I hung on to my credibility.

And, in retrospect, it's a better and more memorable story with that particular ending. Every angler can tell a story (or 94 stories) about the one that got away. But not many can tell about the one that was landed and dispatched, and *then* got away. ◄∙

beds that exist near a source of incoming fresh water. Finding existing weed beds is no great trick. There's often a cluster of boats around each of the best. A depth-finder is a handy tool for exploring in search of more isolated beds. I've found many by simply drifting and peering down with my polarized sunglasses or while trolling, when my hook finds them for me.

There is a large bay on the lake where my family cottage is located. It encompasses perhaps 3 or 4 square miles of water and averages about 10 feet in depth. Most often, the walleye are found in the "main" lake, which has an average depth of about 40 feet. But on dark, rainy days, or at night, they will come into this bay.

Within the bay are two distinct weed beds, each of which occupies only about 300 square feet of real estate, a tiny fraction of the entire bay. Yet we have caught hundreds of walleye and other game fish from these two beds and probably less than ten or so from any other part of the bay. It's further proof of the old adage that 95 percent of the fish are found in 5 percent of the water.

With the right tackle and approach (which are covered in detail in subsequent chapters), working weeds need not be a pain. If you avoid them, you will be making a lot of fish very happy.

Shoals, Humps, and Submerged Islands

Shoals, humps, and submerged islands all indicate a change in depth—sometimes radical—from the surrounding bottom. All can be fish magnets.

Shoals can be as small as a handful of rocks or boulders or may encompass hundreds or thousands of square feet. Crayfish and small fish take shelter among the nooks and crannies. Big fish go there to eat them. *You* should go there to offer your appetizer.

Luckily for us, many shoals can be readily identified by the floating marker buoys used to warn boaters. These buoys tell powerboaters, water-skiers, and sailors to "stay away."

But they beckon anglers with a wink and a promise.

Not all shoals are marked, of course. Some are too small and tight to shore, others are deep enough not to pose a hazard. Many can be found simply by looking at a shoreline and picturing the geographical features that continue under the water. Many points extend out under the surface, too, and rockslides on shore usually continue under the water.

▶ **Most shoals are best fished under low-light or high-wave conditions.**

Cast shallow or medium-diving crank baits (more on these in chapter 3), and work them from shallow to deep. If the fish aren't on top or on the sides, work the surrounding, deeper water to see if you can get them "at home."

Humps are exactly what they sound like, bumps or saddles rising up from a uniform bottom. They can be the size of a desk or as big as a house. The larger ones qualify as submerged islands.

Some may rise high enough to encourage weed growth when the surrounding water has none. Many collect more baitfish-attracting rubble on top than the surrounding water (often a selection of lures from unwary trollers).

All of them serve as feeding areas for game fish or as landmarks for their feeding routes, some even as home bases. Humps will offer shade along their sides during high light penetration days, as well.

Graphs are very valuable for finding humps, especially small ones (see

Humps, even small ones, often hold some fish.

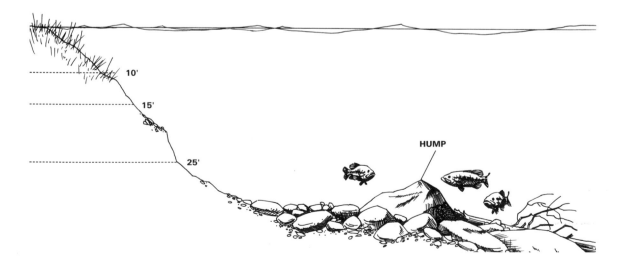

10'

15'

25'

HUMP

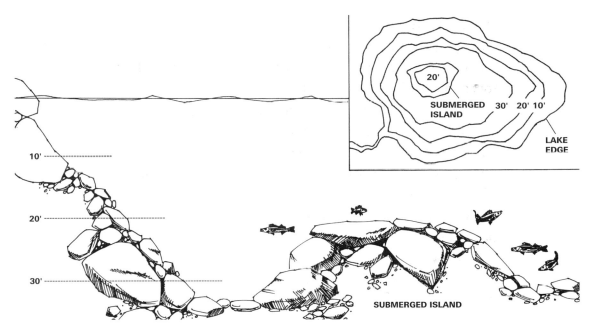

Submerged islands, by nature of their larger size, can host larger populations of fish than can be found near humps (see illustration opposite), but they are often well-known angling hot spots.

chapter 6 for more information). Contour maps may show the largest of them, and those that rise close enough to the surface may be marked by buoys.

I've found many by accident, usually while drifting or trolling a bottom-bouncing rig. Often a small hump will produce the only fish within a very large area. Finding one is like discovering one more Christmas present under the pile of wrappings.

Flats, Shelves, and Drop-Offs

Picture an arena with descending tiers of seats leading to a flat playing surface. Now turn it upside down, immerse it in a lake, and you've got a terrific fishing spot.

The top of your inverted arena is called a "flat." Few flats have tiers, or ledges, on all sides. Usually they extend from shore, and the tiers, steps, or ledges go down to deeper water on one or two sides, sometimes three.

Most of the best flats have at least some weed growth that sustains a population of forage fish. Under low-light and/or high-wave conditions, game fish can be found on top of the flat. If weed growth is heavy enough, they may stay there under high light penetration periods, as well.

The lake where our family has a cottage is a deep, clear, lake with a good population of walleye and smallmouth bass. It also holds some largemouth and pike.

My favorite spot is a flat much as I described above, with sparse to medium-heavy weed growth bracketed on two sides by shoals. The top of the flat is about 11 to 13 feet deep. The tiers, or ledges, leading to deep water are fairly wide. The first one is in 15 feet of water, the second at about 20 feet. If the walleye aren't on top, we'll usually find them along one of the ledges. The smallies are usually on top, near the shoals or hugging the first ledge.

On days with low light penetration, walleye often can be found on top of the flat or along the first breakline at the 15-foot mark. On sunnier days, they usually drop down to the next tier, at 20 feet, or occasionally even deeper. Smallmouth bass are usually on the flat, focused toward the rocky shoals on either end. My preferred angling method is drifting (if the wind is right) or back-trolling with a floating worm or floating jig-head rig along the length of the first and second breaklines. If the fish are on top, I like to drift and cast, usually with jigs.

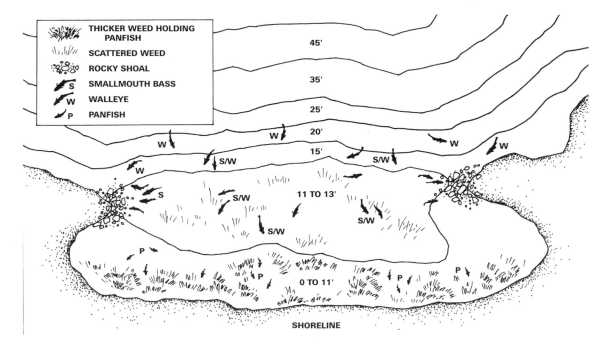

▶ **A long edge leading to a depth change is called a "breakline." The area where weeds end and a different bottom begins can also be called a break or breakline. Several ledges parallel to each other, each descending deeper, are a series of breaklines. A steep, sheer, single break is a "drop-off."**

All breaks and breaklines are not created equal when it comes to holding fish. If you look at a hydrographic map, you can easily spot the breaklines. Some bend inward, some bend outward.

Inward bending lines indicate more abrupt changes in depth (A in the illustration below). If this occurs near a feeding zone, fish may use it as a shortcut from their home to food and back. Some of the outward-bending breaks (B, C) may be wide enough to form a deeper sort of flat. Again, if relatively close to food, and if offering a comfortable temperature, these deeper flats or wider breaks may hold a school of resting "at home" fish.

I like these spots a lot!

Sharp drop-offs are my least favorite areas to fish, but if they satisfy the "safe" and "near food" criteria, they will often hold some fish, which will usually be suspended. These fish are not relating to bottom, but rather they "suspend" at some point between the surface and bottom.

Tightly spaced lines on contour maps (A) mark abrupt depth changes (drop-offs). Lines spaced farther apart (B, C) indicate less abrupt changes in depth: these wider breaks, which nearly form flats, are often the home area for a variety of game fish. D is interesting because its narrowness indicates a travel route. E offers the deepest hole, or possible resting area, in a relatively large section of the lake.

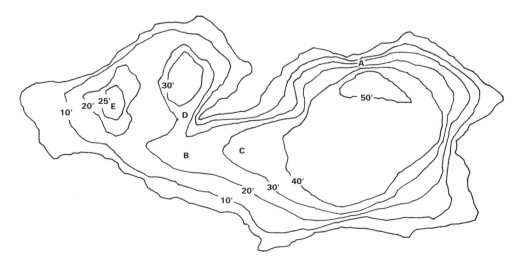

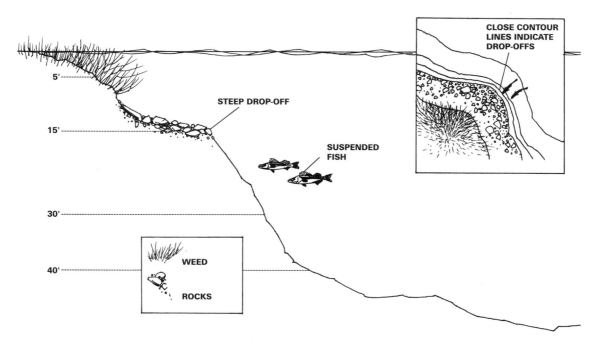

If near feeding zones, drop-offs will sometimes hold fish. Usually, though, the fish are suspended (not relating to bottom) and can be tricky to pinpoint.

Learning about a lake can be much like forming a relationship. It's not often love at first sight. It takes time to sense its moods, to learn where it likes to be fished and where fishing is unproductive, to know whether a delicate, feather-like approach is called for or a bolder, more aggressive—Hey! Is it just me or is it getting a tad warm in here?

CHAPTER **3**

OK, We Found Them—Now What?

It's time to discuss tackle and tactics.

▶ **Use tackle suitable for the species you're after and the water in which it's found.**

You don't wear a tuxedo to a football game. You don't use a hammer to repair a watch. You don't use a muskie rod to catch sunfish. And you can cast a surface popper all day long and not catch a single catfish.

If you are a beginning angler, a good all-round outfit starts with a $6^{1}/_{2}$- to 7-foot medium-action, graphite-composite rod. Match it with a medium-light spinning reel spooled with quality 8-pound test monofilament line. Unless otherwise indicated, this is the outfit I refer to in the pages to come. (See the primer in the appendix for more information on rods and reels.)

Depending on the conditions, you can have fun catching fish from under a pound to over 20 pounds with this setup.

As I mentioned earlier, you needn't break the bank on your rod and reel, particularly if it's your first outfit. Buy good quality—but you don't necessarily need "great" quality. A decent combo will cost $75 to $150. With the money you save, you can afford premium-quality line and hooks, where it pays to spend a little more.

Most people who work in tackle shops fish, too. Describe your needs and your budget. Because they rely so much on repeat business, chances are they'll give you good advice and treat you right. Department stores often have decent prices and equipment, but their staff, overall, isn't as knowledgeable.

If you're new to the fishing game, build a relationship with an established tackle shop. You won't be sorry.

▶ **Learn to tie a reliable knot for connecting your terminal tackle.**

Instructions for tying knots are usually included with the line you purchase. While there are a wide variety of knots you can try, I use the improved

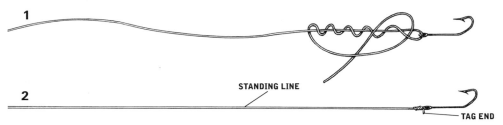

I use the improved clinch knot for almost all my line-to-lure and hook connections. It is a popular knot and, with a little practice, easy to tie. **1.** Pass the line through the hook eye. Double back and make five turns around the standing line. Hold the coils in place, thread the end of the line around the first loop above the eye, and then thread them through the big loop. **2.** Hold the tag end and the standing line while you tighten the coils. Take care that the coils don't "jump" over each other. Slide tight against the eye. Clip the tag end.

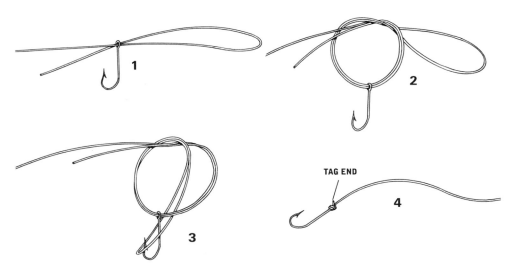

The Palomar knot is another strong, reliable knot. It's easy to learn, but it's a little bulky and is most useful for attaching bare hooks, as big lures with treble hooks are difficult to pass through the loop this knot requires. **1.** Double about 4 inches of the line and pass the loop through the hook eye. **2.** Let the hook hang loose and tie an overhand knot in doubled line. Avoid twisting the lines, and don't tighten the knot. **3.** Pull the loop of line far enough to pass it over the hook. Make sure the loop passes completely over this attachment. **4.** Pull both the tag end and the standing line to tighten. Clip the tag end.

clinch knot most of the time. Properly tied, it won't fail you. Some people prefer the Palomar knot. With few exceptions, and particularly when using live bait, tie your hook or lure directly to your line.

A couple of exceptions: Ball-bearing snap swivels are necessary when repeatedly casting or trolling spinners. They will help eliminate the dreaded line twist (more about that later). And if you are targeting large, toothy critters like pike or muskie, you may wish to attach your offering to a 6- to 18-inch steel or braided wire leader.

In most other instances, however, the KISS rule applies (Keep It Simple Stupid). Snaps and swivels make changing lures and hooks easier, but they can impede the action of some lures and add unnecessary clutter. The more natural a bait or lure looks, the more likely it is to fool fish.

Bait Fishing

Most fishermen use, or have used, bait to catch fish for these simple and persuasive reasons: a few hooks, sinkers, and a container of worms costs less and is more portable than a bulging tackle box; bait fishing is easier and more relaxing than using hardware or flies; bait fishing works.

▸ **Properly presented, bait will catch anything with fins.**

The word "presentation" is going to come up a lot in these pages. After locating your fish, how you present your offering is of paramount importance.

With bait, for the most part, proper presentation means using small hooks, light line, and minimal weight.

Small hooks will catch more fish than large ones. Too many neophytes gob a worm onto a gaff-sized hook. Small or yearling fish won't be deterred. They'll peck the worm right off, with little likelihood of being hooked. Larger fish will eye the contraption warily and dismiss it with a disdainful sniff. Fish are dumb, but not *that* dumb.

I've caught salmon and carp over 20 pounds on hooks the size of my pinkie fingernail. Small hooks are less likely to impair the movement of live bait and are easier to hide in all kinds of bait.

Light line (8 lb. test or less) reduces water drag and is less visible to the fish. Minimal weight allows for freer movement and is less likely to trigger a fish's "this ain't normal" alarm when it picks up the bait.

▶ **Exception: High, fast water, with big fish the quarry, obviously calls for heavier tackle. So does fishing in dense cover such as heavy weeds or timber. You will still hook more fish on lighter gear, but you won't land many, and those you do land may be unfit for release due to exhaustion. Use common sense and match your tackle to the situation.**

NOT-SO-TALL TALE

The Billy Goat

n my middle and late teens I discovered girls. For a time, their appeal even outstripped that of a brown trout. When I was about seventeen, a friend and I would often hitchhike for a few days at a time in "cottage country" a hundred or so miles to the north. We did it for the sense of adventure. (The fact that we found a girls' camp once or twice might have had a bit to do with it, too.) We slept wherever darkness found us: at the sides of roads, in fields, even in graveyards once or twice. I loved not knowing where I'd be unrolling my sleeping bag from one night to the next. We traveled lightly, without a tent, and with very little money, but I did often pack a fishing rod and some gear.

One morning, we spent most of our last dollar on toast and coffee at a roadside diner–general store–bait shop–gas station. It was situated where two lakes met on a small, two-lane highway. We were glumly discussing the necessity of heading home when my friend suggested I catch some fish to trade for supplies. We approached the owner with the idea,

and he was amenable. He told us of a dam about 5 miles down a dirt side road that was a popular spot for catching brook trout (also called speckled trout or specs in our neck of the woods). Our last 25 cents went into his pocket to pay for a dozen worms.

There was little traffic and we had to walk the whole way, but when we found the dam we knew the owner hadn't fibbed. It *was* popular. There were about twenty people fishing there, pretty much evenly split between fishing directly below the dam and about 50 yards away, in a large pool that eventually emptied into a lake.

My friend didn't fish, and, in any event, we only had the one outfit. He said he'd cheer me on, which meant he found a shady spot and napped. The area below the dam was too crowded, so I made my way down to the large pool and joined the people there.

An hour passed and I was fishless, as were the others. The below-dam crowd seemed to be doing just as poorly. I kept turning my attention to the 50 yards of water that separated the two

Since we know that most fish spend most of their time on or near bottom (just trust me, OK?), that's where your bait should be. In moving water, using the current (as discussed in chapter 1) is the best method of presentation.

Sometimes big fish, especially migratory trout and salmon, will rest in deep, slow-moving pools. Usually, there is still *some* current, and bait can be presented on the bottom with little or no weight or just above it by suspending it under a float. Often, these fish have been worked over by a host of

groups of anglers. It was a stretch of boulder-strewn rapids, with lots of churning whitewater between and around the boulders. No one was fishing there. It looked dangerous.

After another hour of fruitless fishing, I decided that it didn't look *that* dangerous. I was young, fit, reasonably agile, and not overly bright. So I carefully made my way from shore, hopping from boulder to boulder. Along the way I found what I'd hoped I would. Every third or fourth rock I landed on was large enough to create a small pocket of relatively quiet water behind it.

I dunked my worm into one such pocket and seconds later had a nice 12-inch brookie. The next hour or so was as much fun as I'd ever had. And I probably used up a decent portion of my lifetime supply of luck, too. Like a sure-footed billy goat, I dashed from rock to rock, back to shore to deposit a fish with my friend, and back to the rapids again. Every pocket I tried had a fish in it. I only had to use a portion of a worm. The fish were used to reacting quickly as the current sped food

past them. They would hit immediately. The legal limit was generous back then (the late 1960s). I was allowed 15 specs, or 10 pounds plus 1 fish.

In fairly short order, I had a dozen specs from 10 to 13 inches. And not a single one of the other fishermen, who all watched my success, followed suit. I remarked on this to my friend as we headed back to the main road. He said, "Yeah, *they* must be nuts," and laughed like a loon.

The storekeeper was as good as his word. We traded ten of the specs for bread, peanut butter, soft drinks, chocolate bars, and cigarettes. (Did I mention I wasn't overly bright back then?) He also promised a breakfast on the house the next morning.

We cooked the remaining two fish over a campfire that evening. And they *would* have been good too, if they hadn't kept falling into the fire as we tried to prop them up on sticks. We had to settle for charred-on-the-outside-sushi-on-the-inside. But, all in all, it was one of the most memorable experiences of my life. ◄◄

anglers and have learned to ignore the most delicate presentation of roe, worms, and single eggs.

This situation is one of the reasons why I regularly give thanks to the anonymous angler who first used a hypodermic syringe to inject air into a worm, turning a sinking bait into a floating one. Now, of course, worm "blowers" are available at any tackle shop and are an essential part of my equipment.

I inject a small worm and pinch on just enough weight (about 8 to 10 inches above the hook) to sink it. I toss the worm into the head of the pool and it s-l-o-w-l-y tumbles to the deep resting area and stops. At least the sinker stops. The worm, instead of sitting on the bottom where it is easily ignored, is now undulating right in front of the noses of those fish.

The impertinence! Many of these brutes have gotten downright annoyed and decided to teach my worm some respect—much to my delight.

▶ **Fish are either in an aggressive, neutral, or negative mood.**

A stationary approach is fine when you are "on" feeding fish or working an area they are passing through.

A moving presentation is required if you are trying to find fish or trying to trigger a strike from a neutral or negative fish. You can move your bait by casting and retrieving, drifting, or trolling.

Casting is best if you are working over a relatively small piece of structure, such as a small shoal, an isolated clump of weeds, or a dock. It's obviously your only option if you are shore-bound.

A slow retrieve is usually best with bait. Remember the smells-good-and-looks-harmless rule and the fish's uncanny sense of what's "normal" or not. A slowly retrieved bait, or even a stationary one, attracts interest. A fast retrieve may provoke suspicion or even alarm.

Drifting in a boat is a fine way to cover water. A slow to medium drift in the right direction lets you work flats and breaklines. A very slow drift means you can cast, and each cast covers slightly different water. A too-fast drift can often be controlled by judicious use of your outboard, an electric motor, or a wind sock. (A wind sock is like a collapsible parachute that drags in the water, slowing a boat's drift.)

Trolling is best on still or low-wind days or when you want precise control of where your bait is going. Back-trolling in these conditions, with a small outboard (15 hp or less) in reverse, is my favorite method for covering deeper (15 feet plus) water. Larger boats with bigger outboards require an electric motor and can forward troll. Forward trolling with an outboard, even a small one, usually means you'll move too fast for a live-bait presentation.

▶ **Back-trolling not only means moving quietly and more slowly, but it also allows for quicker, more precise turns when following contours. Your line is more directly beneath you, rather than far behind as is the case with traditional forward trolling. Less line out means it's easier to detect pickups and there's less stretch when it's hook-setting time.**

My favorite live-bait, big-water rig is an injected dew worm (night crawler) hooked once in the nose on a short-shanked #8 or #10 hook. It rides about 18 inches above a half-ounce egg or walking-type sinker, held in place with a small split shot.

Thread your line through the egg sinker first and then peg it in place with your shot. Tie on your hook, bait up, and you're ready.

The heavy egg sinker should always be in contact with the bottom, your worm or minnow riding above it. Your sinker is important, as it telegraphs all sorts of helpful information to the discerning angler: the type of bottom, changes in depth, the presence of humps, and so on.

When a fish bites, it's usually best to release line immediately. As the fish carries the bait off, all it feels is the small shot sinker; the heavy, alarm-producing egg sinker stays on the bottom. For this reason, I always drift or troll with the bail of my reel open, keeping my line from spilling out by holding

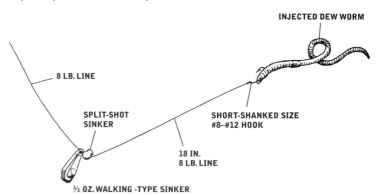

I usually use this basic slip-sinker rig while drifting or back-trolling. It is especially effective for walleye and smallmouth bass.

INJECTED DEW WORM

8 LB. LINE

SPLIT-SHOT SINKER

SHORT-SHANKED SIZE #8–#12 HOOK

18 IN. 8 LB. LINE

½ OZ. WALKING -TYPE SINKER

it with one finger. When a fish picks up, it's a simple matter to instantly let go of the line.

Sometimes fish will only run a few feet before chowing down. However, fish often carry the bait 25 yards or more before pausing, especially small walleye. Once the fish stops running, close your bail, tighten your slack line, and set the hook. (See pages 130–31 for more information on how to set a hook.)

Obviously, you can't keep your bail open if you're casting and retrieving live bait. In this case, retrieve with your rod held high, at about 11 o'clock. When the fish picks up, you can drop your rod tip to allow for some instant slack while you open your bail.

Floats

Sometimes, the best way to suspend bait just off the bottom is with a float. If the bottom is full of snags or weed-infested, the bottom-bouncing method is frustrating and costly in terms of lost tackle. And float-fishing is just plain fun to boot.

Many of us recall watching those round, red and white bobbers expectantly when we were kids, alert for any twitch and happily ignoring our elders' commands to "wait 'til it goes under."

Small Bait, Large Fish (sometimes)

There's an old angling adage that one should use big bait or lures to catch big fish. My use of worms and roe bags for bait has provided regular exceptions to that rule. Although I usually use night crawlers for my bottom-bouncing rigs, and some of those critters can approach 8 inches long, I regularly catch fish up to 30 pounds on 1-inch garden worms or dime-sized roe bags.

(Roe bags are made by tying 3 or 4 salmon eggs, or 5 to 10 trout eggs, in a soft, colored mesh sack. Occasionally, bits of Styrofoam are added to make the bags float. Low-tech devices, which make the messy job slightly less messy, are available at tackle shops. More roe details later.)

Small garden worms are just the ticket for smallish trout and panfish, but they can also be dynamite for tempting big, migratory fish like steelhead and salmon, especially when you are faced with tough, clear-water conditions.

Of course, some of those floats were big enough to raise the *Titanic,* and nothing could fully immerse them. But there was, and still is for me, a special magic in seeing a float motionless on the water one second and gone the next.

Most anglers today have abandoned the round plastic floats in favor of the pencil-style floats popularized in Europe. These are constructed primarily of balsa wood, Styrofoam, or light, hollow plastic. Some sensitive ones are still made from porcupine quills. Every angler should carry an assortment of sizes.

As with hooks, follow the Smallest-That-Will-Do-The-Job maxim. If fishing slow-moving water, use smaller, lighter floats. Bigger-bodied floats that can be heavily weighted should be used to combat fast-water conditions. On lakes and ponds, wind conditions, the size of your quarry, and the size of your bait will dictate the size of your float.

If you're fishing for pike or largemouth with 5-inch minnows, you'll need a hefty float to keep the bait from pulling it under. Panfish or small trout call for small bait and lighter floats.

Sometimes wind conditions are such that you'll need to use a larger float than you would prefer just to have weight enough to cast.

▶ **Always use enough weight to "cock" the float—make it stand upright.**

In moving water, attach your shot between float and bait every few inches or feet, with the heaviest directly below the float and the lightest closest to the hook. This allows your bait to drift slightly ahead of your line, so it will be the first thing the fish sees.

Most pencil floats attach to the line with small pieces of rubber tubing that allow for easy

CABELA'S INC.

Pencil floats come in a wide variety of sizes and shapes and are usually attached to the line with rubber tubing (often sold separately—ask your tackle dealer). More streamlined than the old round bobbers, pencil floats are easier to "weight" properly, and fish can tug them down with little resistance. They come in standard or slip (shown) style.

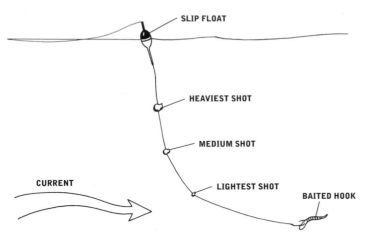

In moving water, it's important to stagger the size of your shot—heaviest shot closest to the float, lightest closest to the hook. This allows your bait to drift slightly ahead of your line, making it the first thing the fish sees.

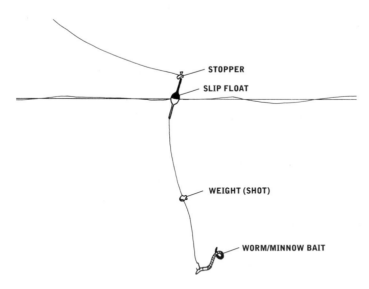

Slip floats let you fish water that is deeper than your rod is long. Slide your line through the hole in the stem of the float, then rig your weight, hook, and bait. Next, tie on or affix your "stopper," either commercial or handmade, at whatever depth you want to fish. The stopper is small enough to be reeled in and cast back through your rod guides. When the float hits the water, the line slides through it until it's stopped by, yes, the stopper.

height adjustments. But what if the fish are 15 feet down and your rod is only 7 feet long? That leaves too much line dangling from the rod tip to cast easily.

Just reach into your vest for those ingenious slip, or sliding, floats. The stopper is tiny enough to slide through the guides of your rod, enabling you to present your bait at much greater depths than the length of your rod allows.

Stoppers are commercially available, but I prefer to make my own. I always carry elastic bands with me for a variety of uses, which I'll detail as we go along. Using a cut piece of thin elastic, I tie a simple overhand knot where I want the float to stop, pulling it very tight. I use nail clippers (another essential piece of gear) to trim the ends. The stopper can be adjusted by pinching and sliding, and it usually lasts for several casts.

Slip floats are worth their weight in gold when you're fishing off a dock or from shore and need to cast into deep water.

Just because you're all grown up now doesn't mean you can't play with floats anymore. There are definitely situations when nothing works better.

Lures

Lures are imitations of baitfish, small fish, or other edible creatures. They are usually constructed of metal (jigs, spinners, spoons), wood or plastic (plugs), or soft plastic (worms, grubs, "critters").

▶ **Presentation is everything when using lures.**

Lures with a built-in action (spinners, plugs, and spoons) operate best at certain speeds and depth ranges. To fish them faster or slower than they were designed for is usually a good way to go home skunked. You can often do a little tinkering to alter depth ranges, though.

Since we are all now *well* aware that most fish spend most of their time on or near bottom (was that a sigh I just heard?), your job is to select the best lure for where *your* fish are.

A deep-diving crank bait is no darn good if bottom is 5 feet down. And I want to be there when a lake trout in 65 feet comes up to smack a surface plug.

Because you've done your homework, you have a fair idea of where your target fish may be and what it likes to eat.

▶ **Usually, fish will eat whatever doesn't pose a threat to them. Smaller fish often form the bulk of a big fish's diet. And because of their opportunistic nature, fish will happily eat crayfish, insects, leeches, frogs, and even cute little baby duckies when they can fit them in.**

Now let's peruse your bulging tackle box to look at the bewildering variety of lures, and discern which are best suited to today's quarry.

Jigs

Jigs are the classic good news–bad news lure. They are the simplest and least expensive type of lure. Composed of a molded lead head with a single hook and dressed with hair, feathers, or the now-popular soft plastic grub, they are the most versatile fish-catchers in the world. With standard spinning gear, jigs can be fished effectively in water from 2 to 30 feet deep.

▶ **A properly presented jig will catch just about anything with fins.**

That's the good news.

The "properly presented" part is the bad news.

No other method of fishing, except fly-fishing, demands more focused concentration on the part of the angler. If you want a jig to twitch, hop, rise, or fall *you* have to twitch it, hop it, lift it, or drop it. (OK, gravity helps a bit with the "falling" part.)

With the addition of a curly-tailed plastic grub, a straight, steady retrieve

How to Do Your Homework

Geographic differences prevent me from being overly specific about the requirements, habits, forage, and location of each species of game fish. Great Lakes brown trout may feed mostly on alewives, whereas those in Arkansas may prefer sculpins. Consequently, the anglers living in each of those areas and targeting those fish would use different bait, lures, and approaches.

But we can thank the Great Angler that we live in the Information Age. I previously mentioned bait and tackle shops as good places for gathering information. Many local newspapers have an outdoor and fishing columnist who writes regularly about area fisheries and angling tactics, and many communities have angling clubs. Most larger newsstands and bookstores carry fishing magazines, often with local information. Check the local library for back issues.

State and provincial fishing regulations are usually updated and printed annually. They are available in most tackle shops, and along with information on slot limits and restrictions, many also indicate the preferences and whereabouts of local game fish.

If you're connected to the Internet, you have enough information at your fingertips to keep your mind boggled for days. Typing your state or province name plus "fish" or "fishing" into any search engine will bring up a host of web addresses to check out. There are probably hundreds of angling clubs and bulletin boards online, many of them local in nature.

You can ask fishing questions at these Internet bulletin boards that other local anglers will often answer. Most of these bulletin board systems save previous "threads" (topics of conversation) under title headings. Newcomers can scan the list of previous threads and often find their topic of interest. Most also have a FAQ (Frequently Asked Questions) section. It often pays to look at the FAQs first.

will account for some fish. But for a jig to work its full fish-catching magic, *you* have to be the magician.

The standard method for fishing a jig is to cast, wait for it to hit bottom, then bring it back to you in a series of hops. The hops can be fast or slow, great sweeps or mere twitches. Lift the tip of your rod, then drop it and retrieve the slack line.

Sounds simple, and it is. The tricky part is detecting the hit.

Jigs come "dressed" with hair or feathers, or you can dress them yourself with bait and/or plastic bodies.

► **Most fish hit on the drop, when your line is momentarily slack.**

Often, you will feel nothing, or what my brother Karl and I call a barely perceptible "tick." (Sometimes, I swear I even *hear* that tick—I know, long time, hot sun, etc.) You have to watch where your line enters the water like your dog watches your fingers when you're eating cheese. Be alert for the slightest twitch or sideways movement. Good polarized sunglasses are a must.

► **At the slightest indication that something is different, set the hook.**

Many times a fish will hit on the initial drop. So close your bail when the jig hits the surface and let it fall on a tight line. Watch that line. Whatever the depth you're fishing, you'll soon sense how long it takes to hit bottom, where your line will slacken. You might find it helpful to "count" your line down to the bottom to get a more precise feel for when your jig will get there. If, on your third cast, your line slackens 2 seconds sooner than it normally takes to hit bottom—*set that hook!*

I've seen amazing underwater footage of bass completely inhaling and then spitting out a lure without the angler having a clue that something just happened. Bass are masters at this, and walleye and other species are no slouches, either.

So anything that encourages a fish to hang onto the jig for an extra second is more likely to bring it to your boat. Soft, scented plastic bodies on jigs are a boon to anglers because they feel more natural, and fish will often hold them a little longer—a *little* longer. You still have to stay alert and become a compulsive line-watcher. I often add a piece of worm, a minnow, or a strip of perch fillet to my jig as an added enticement for the fish to hit and "stay" a while.

Dunking jigs in shallow, weedy water can be dynamite. Karl and I will drift over a weed bed, and using only 6 to 10 feet of line, drop our jigs into pockets between weeds or along edges. Depending on the wind, sometimes we only get one drop, sometimes two or three, before lifting up and waiting for the next opening to appear. Hits are instinctive and often jarring, especially if it's a 15-pound muskie or 6-pound walleye on 6 feet of line!

Part of what makes this type of jigging so much fun is that we're looking almost straight down in shallow water, so we occasionally *see* the bass, walleye, or muskie dart from under a clump of weeds to inhale the jig. Sometimes I'm so awestruck that I fail to set the hook in time. My brain freezes at the thought of how a jig can be *there* and then, in a split-second blur of fins, *not be there,* only to reappear when the fish spits it out.

It's easy to experiment with jigs. So don't be afraid to vary your retrieve and its speed. I often watched an angler on our home lake who caught a lot of walleye by holding his rod low to the water, retrieving his jig in a series of three quick twitches with a slight pause between.

I like to hold my rod high and do my "hops" by retrieving quickly for a couple of turns, pausing, reeling slowly for a turn, and then quickly again. This way, my line is rarely completely slack, and I can detect pickups well. But often I do the "classic" one or two quick upward twitches, retrieve slack as I lower the rod tip, and repeat.

▶ **Changing speeds can be very important when using jigs.**

Slow, crawling retrieves work well after a cold front when fish are sluggish. A quick, jerky retrieve may trigger a strike from a neutral or negative fish, which might ignore a slow retrieve.

I like to jig with a fairly stiff 6- to 7-foot rod with a sensitive tip, using 6- to 8-pound line when fishing deep, clear water. When dunking in cover, the same rod will do, but I'll use 10- to 14-pound line.

Jigs come in a wide variety of sizes, shapes, and colors. Tiny $^1/_{32}$- to $^1/_{16}$-ounce jigs are great for panfish, $^1/_8$- to $^1/_2$-ounce jigs are popular for bass, walleye, trout, pike, and muskie. Even heavier jigs can be used for plumbing greater depths or combating very fast water.

It takes time, patience, and concentration to become a confident jigger. But if I were ever restricted to using only one type of artificial lure on any given body of water, I would happily choose jigs.

> *Jigs*
> ▶ *Favorite head colors: black, white, gray, yellow, chartreuse*
> ▶ *Favorite body colors: black, white, pumpkinseed, yellow, smoke, chartreuse, motor oil, purple*
> ▶ *Species: panfish, bass, walleye, trout, salmon, pike, and muskie*

Spinners

A spinner is a metal lure with a straight shaft around which a blade "spins" when drawn through the water. They usually have one set of treble hooks (Mepps) or a single hook (Erie Dearie). Like most lures, spinners come in an astonishing array of colors and sizes, and most tackle shops would like you to have three of each.

▶ **Spinners should be attached to your line with a quality ball-bearing snap swivel to retard (but not completely eliminate) line twist.**

Spinners are designed to work on a straight retrieve and also can be trolled. They're easy to use and will catch fish. I'm not sure what spinners are supposed to represent to game fish—perhaps another fish. But it doesn't matter as long as they work.

Spinner blades produce both sound and vibration, which fish can hear and sense through their lateral line. This makes them ideal for fishing

MAGIC PORTRAITS

Some spinners come with bucktail attached. The effectiveness of others can often be improved by adding bait. The long, single-hooked Erie Dearie (center) is a favorite for fishing sparse to medium-thick weeds.

murky water. Long, thin-bladed spinners run deeper than wider-bladed versions but don't produce as much vibration.

Spinners work at any speed as long as it's fast enough to rotate the blade. In moving water, they can be cast to the head of a pool and retrieved down and across.

Remember the pool where I persuaded those jaded trout to smack my floating worm? Well, Karl would provoke those same fish with a well-presented spinner.

I've seen it many times. Migratory trout and salmon that have been ignoring artfully presented bait or flies all day will savagely smash a spinner, often on consecutive casts. I like to call this the Monty Python Rule: Every once in a while you should offer the fish something "completely different."

Spinners are good for fishing at a variety of depths. You can retrieve them quickly when "buzzing" the top of a weed bed, or with some added weight, they can be effectively trolled as deep as 20 feet or more.

The main drawback to the traditional Mepps-style spinner is its uncanny ability to find and attach itself to any rock, tree, or weed in the area. I've left a lot of souvenirs on the bottoms of lakes and rivers over the years. The single-hooked Erie Dearie–type, as I mentioned earlier, is excellent for fishing sparse to medium-thick weed cover.

Eventually, even if you are using a quality ball-bearing snap swivel, spinners will twist your line. This twisting weakens your line, shortens your casts, and inevitably forms a spaghetti-like tangled mess. Luckily, it's easy to fix *before* it gets to that point. Be alert, because it's definitely hard to repair once you have a bird's nest of twisted line.

First, remove all terminal tackle. If you're fishing moving water, let the current carry your bare line downstream until you are no longer feeding out twisted line. Immerse your rod tip if you have to, to get the line to sink. In a few minutes the current will work out the twist.

If boating, simply troll forward, feeding out bare line until you're well past the twisted part, close the bail, and

Spinners
▶ *Favorite colors: black, black and yellow, black and chartreuse, silver, brass, gold*
▶ *Species: all*

wait a bit. This is my cue to light my pipe, pour a cup of coffee, admire the scenery, and ponder some of life's deeper questions, such as "What color should I try next?"

Spoons

Spoons are curved pieces of metal that vaguely resemble their namesakes and wobble through the water like injured minnows. Some are heavy and designed for casting, trolling, or jigging. Some are feather-light and are usually attached to a downrigger. (See chapter 6 for more on downriggers.) Most spoons come with one set of treble hooks, some with a single hook. They can be an effective lure for most game fish, but I use them primarily for trout and salmon in open water (lakes and river mouths).

Like spinners, spoons are easy to use and can be fished effectively at a variety of depths. Most spoons should be fished at a medium-slow speed. If you reel or troll too quickly, their seductive I'm-Helpless wobble will turn into a sort of scary spin, and pretty soon you've got that line twist thing happening again (and no fish to boot). Some spoons have very little curve and can be fished at higher speeds. Always take a look at your spoon when it nears the boat or before trolling to make sure the speed looks good.

Although mostly used with a traditional straight retrieve, spoons can be effectively jigged. Ice fishermen always have an assortment of spoons, and deep, vertical jigging with heavy spoons can trigger hits from salmon and lake trout. The flash and flutter

MAGIC PORTRAITS

Light, thin "flutter" spoons (bottom) are usually fished with a downrigger (see chapter 6). The single, Siwash hook on these spoons holds giant salmon better than the traditional treble hooks. Thicker, heavier spoons (top) are designed for casting or trolling with normal angling equipment.

Spoons
▶ *Favorite colors: silver, gold, brass, chartreuse, silver and blue, silver and green, gold and red*
▶ *Species: primarily trout, salmon, pike*

of a jerked, then tumbling spoon will attract fish from farther away than will a traditional lead-head jig.

Although some spoons come with a split ring attached, many don't. I believe all should, so I attach my own to all my spoons. When casting spoons, I tie my line directly to the split ring, which I then attach to the lure. (Tying your knot directly to the lure impairs the side-to-side wobble of spoons and some plugs.) When trolling, I'll use a snap swivel.

Split rings are tiny, tightly coiled, round bits of steel. (See the primer in the appendix for more detail.) They are adept at stabbing you in that tender area under the thumbnail and then launching themselves into orbit before you can exact revenge. If you are one of those rare anglers devoid of a masochistic streak, you can buy split ring pliers at most tackle shops. Allegedly, they make the task easier.

I wouldn't know.

A small selection from the wide variety of plugs. From top to bottom on left: minnow imitators, divers or "crank baits," and a lipless crank. From top to bottom on right: "banana" baits and a wobbler, followed by surface plugs.

Plugs

There is a wider variety of plugs to choose from than all other lures combined. Most plugs resemble a minnow or baitfish.

Some float. Some float, then dive. Some float, then dive, then stay put. Some sink. Some sink, then dive deeper. Some are painted so realistically that you're tempted to fillet them. Others resemble nothing ever seen outside a Salvador Dalí nightmare.

Some are smaller than your thumb, some as long as your forearm, and most are in between. Some shimmy, others wobble. Some rattle, others gurgle. They have two, three, even four sets of treble hooks.

They are *all* expensive and are all adept at catching anglers' wallets. Most of them will catch a fish sometimes. Some of them will catch a lot of fish, a lot of the time.

I'll try to focus on those.

Minnow-Style Plugs

If I were restricted to only one type of plug, it would be the long, narrow, minnow-imitating plugs popularized by Rapala. Excellent ones are now available from a variety of manufacturers, as well.

The basic model is 3 to 5 inches long and floats at rest, dives a few inches upon retrieve, and floats back up if paused. Its natural action with a normal retrieve is a tight shimmy, much like a slightly injured minnow.

Fished without weight, especially over weeds, they will tempt bass and pike. With the addition of weight 12 to 15 inches ahead of the lure they can be fished at various depths and for a variety of species.

This lure can be cast or trolled, and one of its best properties is that, when properly tuned, it's effective at *any* speed from a crawl to a muskie-hunting speed-troll.

Although usually perfect right out of the box, sometimes these plugs will track to one side or the other if they've been bounced off rocks or smacked by a few fish. Watch your lure as you retrieve it from the water and observe which way it veers. You can make one of these plugs track straight again by bending the nose ring with pliers in the opposite direction from which the lure was veering.

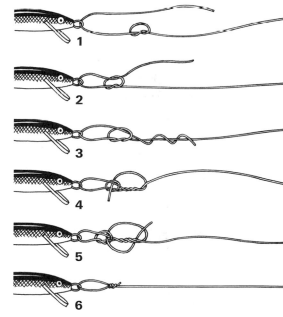

The Rapala knot is designed to give free rein to the natural shimmy of its namesake minnow imitators. I prefer to attach a split ring to the lure and then tie an improved clinch knot (see page 30) to the ring.

Some manufacturers recommend using a loop-type (Rapala) knot for attaching these plugs, while some anglers like a tight clinch-style knot tied to the bottom third of the nose ring. I prefer to attach a split ring (ouch) and tie my knot to it.

A relatively recent, and very exciting, variation of this type of plug has been making a splash. Loosely referred to as "jerk" plugs or "jerk baits," they have been given a slightly bigger lip and made to be neutrally buoyant. They float at rest, dive a few feet upon retrieve, and, if paused, stay absolutely motionless.

They don't go up.

They don't go down.

They don't *go*.

Many game fish seem to love this sort of thing. Brother Karl has had some banner, multispecies days using jerks. He'll cast the lure, sweep his rod savagely to make it dive, pause, retrieve his slack, jerk again, pause, etc. As with jigs, fish often hit on the pause. Although the lure only dives to about 5 feet, Karl has had walleye come up from 15 feet or more to crunch it.

A chronic arm injury prevents me from using them this way, but I've had success retrieving quickly, pausing, and retrieving quickly again.

On one occasion, Karl and I were drifting and casting for salmon and trout at the mouth of a feeder creek on Lake Ontario. We usually use heavy-bodied spoons like the Little Cleo or narrow, deep, heavy plugs like the Rattlin' Spot. Karl had hooked and landed a 35-pound chinook that hit his Spot. On a whim, I tied on a 7-inch Rapala Husky Jerk, a lure I normally use for walleye, bass, and pike. On my third cast I had a smashing hit, and twenty minutes later I landed a twin to Karl's fish. (Find out more about this method in chapter 9.)

These jerk lures can also be effectively trolled, and you can add to your success ratio by occasionally sweeping the rod forward then dropping it back.

I can't think of a single species of freshwater game fish that won't hit these minnow-imitating plugs at some time

Minnow-Style Plugs
▶ *Favorite colors: silver, gold, sliver and black, gold and black, silver and blue, perch, chub*
▶ *Species: all*

or other. They can be fished at most depths and at virtually any speed. These plugs deserve space in every angler's tackle box.

Diving Plugs

Diving plugs, usually called crank baits, are minnow or baitfish imitators characterized by the exaggerated "lips," which protrude from the front of the lures. They usually float at rest and, depending on the size and angle of the lip, will dive from 3 to 20 feet or more during the retrieve. Shallow to medium divers can be effectively cast and retrieved; the deepest divers work best when trolled. They work well at all but the fastest speeds.

Body styles range from slim to chunky, and they come in the now-familiar astonishing array of sizes and colors.

The lip on this type of lure does more than just allow it to dive to various depths. It also acts as a fairly effective guard against snags or bouncing off rocks and other debris. If you do get hung up, just slackening the line will often allow the lure to float free. This is a blessing for the income-challenged angler because these lures don't come cheap.

Crank baits are perfect for working from shallow to deeper water, as you would when checking out a shoal or steep break. Starting your retrieve slowly keeps the lure at a relatively shallow depth, and you can speed up the retrieve as water depth increases.

These lures are an excellent choice when working weed-free flats with sandy, muddy, or pebbly bottoms. Use a diver that just ticks the bottom. The industrious wiggle, combined with the commotion the lip makes as it churns up bits of bottom will attract the attention of any game fish in the area.

Crank baits are probably the fastest-growing segment of the lure-making industry. Average anglers and seasoned pros love the way these lures can quickly cover water and trigger strikes from any aggressive fish in the vicinity. They are tailor-made for walleye and smallmouth bass, but just about any game fish will take a poke at them.

Many cranks, along with the minnow-style lures discussed earlier, now come with built-in rattles. But my personal jury is hung on this topic.

> *Diving Plugs*
> ▶ *Favorite colors: silver,*
> *gold, silver and black, gold*
> *and black, silver and blue,*
> *perch, chub, crayfish, and*
> *shad*
> ▶ *Species: all*

In stained water, I believe the rattle can be helpful in "calling" fish. And I like a rattle in jerk baits, where it is activated when jerked and silent when paused. The intermittent aspect may be intriguing to fish.

But I also think the addition of rattles to an already-aggressive lure can make all but the most active fish shy away. Most fish prefer easy pickings, and I have some reservations about something that looks *and* sounds like the Tasmanian Devil. A rattling crank certainly would be my last choice of lure for skittish fish or those sulking after a cold front. But it would be my first pick for quickly covering an area to find active, aggressive fish.

Wobbling Plugs

For the sake of simplicity, I'll narrow this category to two types of lure. There's the exaggerated "banana" type, like Flatfish or Lazy Ike, and the more streamlined style, like a Beno or the venerable Creek Chub.

The banana type has a slow, tantalizing, side-to-side wobble that mournfully declares, "I am helpless and without hope. Please eat me." A lot of fish find this sort of offer very appealing. These lures *must* be fished slowly, and weight usually needs to be added to the line to cast as far as you want and/or to reach the depth you want.

These plugs can be frustrating to cast, especially into a wind, because they are adept at tangling themselves. (Even out of the water, they kind of have that "inept" thing going.)

They are best trolled or drifted slowly. I prefer the ones that float at rest, and I attach a weight about 18 inches above the lure. I've had great success with walleye and bass by back-trolling them at a crawl in 15 to 20 feet of water. In one experiment, we found that with 6-pound test line, $1/2$-ounce sinkers, and a slow troll we could catch lake trout at a little over 30 feet.

The more streamlined wobbler still has a sexy sashay but can be fished at a higher speed. This lets you cover more water and may trigger strikes

Muskie Mania

Every group of friends has a member who is "out there." Most organizations have their lunatic fringe. Every family has a weird uncle or a grandparent who is no longer in the "here and now."

But they are our friends or family. We care about them and care for them.

Which brings me to the muskie fisherman.

Muskie maniacs are a breed apart. Their rods have the flexibility of pool cues. They use $400 bait-casting reels that are always filled with the newest "super" line. They all have forearms like Popeye from wrestling with their lures, never mind the fish.

They have two basic facial expressions. The first is a weird grimace accompanied by a crazed gleam in the eye. This represents anticipation, laced with a generous dollop of pain (*you* try hurling those monstrous lures for ten straight hours). The second is a haunted, ghastly, glazed look that comes after yet another 40-plus-pounder follows the lure to the boat, poses for a mental snapshot, and then disappears.

If you see muskie fishermen plying their trade, spare them a kind thought. Give them plenty of room. Don't wave. They have enough problems.

---

from neutral fish that ignore the pathetic meandering of the banana lure. The bodies of these lures are often jointed, sometimes more than once, giving them a snaky look in the water.

These lures usually sink and may not require extra weight, depending on your speed of retrieve and just how deep you want to be. The streamlined wobblers, along with the minnow type, come in the widest variety of sizes, from tiny to truly intimidating.

The largest of these, the 8- to 20-inch behemoths, are obviously aimed at the muskie, pike, or big-walleye special-ist. Don't try using these beasts with standard spinning gear unless, of course, you've always wondered what operating a jackhammer feels like.

Both the banana and streamlined wobblers deserve some space in your tackle box. They appeal to all species, and the banana type is ideal for back-dropping in rivers for migratory fish, as I described back on page 11.

> *Wobbling Plugs*
> ▶ *Favorite banana-style colors: pearl, black, skunk, crayfish, red and white*
> ▶ *Favorite streamlined colors: black, frog, yellow, chub, perch, strawberry*
> ▶ *Species: all*

Surface Plugs

All surface plugs float.

Duh.

Despite this common feature, there is a surprising variety of styles among the "poppers," "crawlers," and "sticks."

Poppers are probably the most versatile and popular of the bunch. As with jigs, *you* impart the action with either occasional twitches or a series of twitches. The hollowed-out front of the popper produces an audible "pop" (surprise!) when twitched. Poppers often have "legs" of rubber, plastic, or feathers and sometimes a "tail" that partially conceals the hook. From the fish's viewpoint, the lure resembles a frog or a similar poor creature obviously close to its expiration date, and therefore an easy meal.

Crawlers or swimmers, like the classic Jitterbug, are usually retrieved steadily, perhaps with the odd pause, and their scooped fronts produce a singsong gurgle and a rocking side-to-side motion. Again, the sound and vibration attracts fish, and the clumsy motion suggests vulnerability.

Stick baits like the Zara Spook are longer and thinner than their surface-plug cousins and don't do much of anything. A few have scooped fronts for sound, but most don't. They just float there, like a . . . like a . . . gimme a sec . . . it'll come to me . . . yeah, that's it! . . . like a stick!

Despite being attention-impaired, stick baits work, or rather, *you* can make them work.

Remember that fish are *always* attuned to their environment, *always* aware of danger and alert to the presence of prey. They will note the stick's initial splash and will eye it warily. When you expertly twitch it or "walk the dog" in a side-to-side motion, the fish doesn't see a stick. It sees a minnow about to join the celestial choir.

The generally accepted rule for all surface plugs is to wait for 30 seconds or more after the cast before doing anything. Let the ripples die away. Up to 50 percent of the time the strike comes after the first twitch.

Bass and surface plugs go together like peanut butter and jelly. Pike will attack them with gusto, as will muskie on occasion. I've even caught decent walleye at night while using a wonderful contraption called a Crazy Crawler. It flails its two metal "wings" and raises a ruckus that can be heard a hundred yards away. It looks like a bat that can't quite get airborne but is still trying desperately.

Surface plugs work best on dead calm water, especially over weeds or deadfall, along shorelines and docks, wherever a bass may lurk. They can also be effective during a light chop, but use a noisier lure or quicken your retrieve to produce a steadier sound the fish can home in on.

Sometimes fish delicately suck in the lure. Other times they smash it. In either instance, it's usually best to wait a heartbeat before setting the hook. The tension can rise so high while anticipating a hit that you must fight the tendency to react as soon as the surface breaks—before the fish has actually hit the lure.

Few things in fishing—heck, few things in *life*—are more exciting than watching the ripples fade away from a twitched lure, only to have the calm shattered by an erupting strike. If you really want to test your pacemaker with Hitchcock-like suspense, fish a surface lure on a moonless night when your eyes can't help you and you're straining all your other senses to the limit . . . waiting . . . waiting . . . waiting . . .

One cautionary note: I learned once, to my horror, that seagulls are attracted to stick baits, too.

> **Surface Plugs**
> ▶ *Favorite colors: Doesn't matter. You are the only one who sees the tops of them. Get a couple with white bellies and couple with dark bellies.*
> ▶ *Species: primarily bass, but also pike, muskie, and panfish*

Combos, Oddballs, and Critters

The effectiveness of some lures can be increased by adding bait or a scented plastic grub. Draping a worm on the hook of a Mepps makes it much more attractive to a walleye. The long, single hook of the Dearie spinner cries out for either a worm or grub.

Adding scents makes sense. (Who groaned?) When a curious fish approaches a whirling spinner, the scent of the worm helps convince it that this strange creature is indeed food. Some lures are specifically designed for the addition of bait, usually live, and are useless without it. The worm harness, for instance, is just a collection of hooks and beads without the worm. And what self-respecting fish wants to eat a harness?

I catch a lot of walleye and smallmouth every year on floating jig heads. These are rigged bottom-bouncing style with egg sinkers, as I described with the injected worm in the Bait Fishing section on page 340. Instead of the hook and worm, I tie on a floating jig head, which is exactly what the name implies. It looks just like a regular jig head, only it's made of painted Styrofoam instead of lead.

They can be fished baited with worms, minnows, leeches, or plastics. Most of the time I use worms, and after years of tinkering, I've developed a method of hooking the worm that works well.

With small jig heads, I'll use half a night crawler hooked just once in the middle. The ends flutter enticingly on either side of the hook. A drawback to this method is the infuriating ease with which yearling bass and panfish steal the worm.

To help combat this I usually use a larger jig head with two half-worms hooked in the middle. The wee fishies might nip one off, but the other often stays on for a bit longer.

Hooking the worm this way puts the trailing edges of the bait just past the business end of the hook, so I am much more likely to make contact when the fish are hitting lightly.

Even at relatively slow speeds, floating jig heads will often spin. By balancing the additional weight of the worm using the above method, you can reduce this tendency. Spinning jig heads not only look unnatural, they will soon twist your line.

I've recently begun experimenting with using soft plastic grub bodies or plastic leeches with floating jig

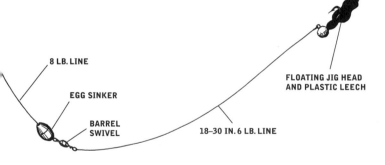

A floating jig-head rig can be very effective for walleye and smallmouth. Favorite "toppings" are a piece of worm, a minnow, a plastic leech (shown here), or a grub/critter. This rig is best fished while drifting or trolling over a relatively clean bottom.

8 LB. LINE

EGG SINKER

BARREL SWIVEL

18–30 IN. 6 LB. LINE

FLOATING JIG HEAD AND PLASTIC LEECH

heads. While I don't get as many hits as I do when using live bait, the fish that do strike are often bigger than average. My blood pressure is also reduced because those 7-inch bass are deterred from stripping the bait with their incessant pecking. I have a love-hate relationship with these yearling smallmouth. I admire their aggression and tenacity but resent feeding them my worms. Sometimes they will trail my offering for a hundred yards, pecking away until one of two things happens: most often they stop because my offering is gone, and I glumly reel in my bare hook. But occasionally I can sense that they suddenly stop in midpeck, and I brace myself. Many times, a nearby walleye or bigger bass has noted the commotion and investigates, resulting in a much happier conclusion for me.

NOT-SO-TALL TALE

Back to Basics

After high school I took a year off to work and travel before going to college. I spent a few months hitchhiking through Europe and saw some great water, but I didn't have a fishing outfit with me. Even if I had, I had no money for hiring guides, renting boats, etc. I settled on a Greek island for a few weeks, living in a cave near a beach on the Ionian Sea. While there, I discovered that I didn't need an outfit to catch fish. I don't recall where I got the line and a couple of hooks. I might have packed them, or I may have scrounged them somewhere.

In any event, the day before I was to leave the island I waded and swam a short distance to a large outcropping of rocks that I liked to just sit on when the heat wasn't too intense. On previous visits I'd noticed that small shellfish clung to the sides, just below the water line. I'd seen locals (there were *no* other tourists on this island at the time except the trio I was traveling with) pry these creatures off the rocks and suck out the contents raw. I had no intention of trying that, but figured if people could eat what lived inside those shells, so might fish.

I pried one loose, dug out the gelatinous contents, and stuck them on a hook. I then lowered it down the side of the rock, holding the line in my hand. Over the next hour I caught several small, brightly colored fish, none larger than 12 inches. I have no idea what they were, and I didn't keep them. When it was time to leave, I balled up the line and hook and tucked it into a tiny crevice in the rock. Every once in a while I like to think it might still be there. The exotic locale, the beautiful colors, and the primitive system I used combine to keep this memory enshrined in my mental scrapbook. ◄

▶ A habit I've formed over the years, and one that I recommend to all anglers, is visualizing what your bait or lure is doing while it's in the water. It helps to paint a mental picture based on the feedback you're getting. A tick off a rock may indicate that you're approaching a ledge. A soft, brief tug tells you of a weed in the area. Lures and sinkers can "talk," and you can learn a lot about the water if you train yourself to listen.

Safety-pin spinners weren't included in the spinner section because, despite the name, they don't spin. Shaped like a V on its side (see accompanying photo), the upper arm has one or two blades that flutter when retrieved or when falling. The bottom arm has a weighted head and single hook, often hidden by a ribbon skirt of plastic or rubber.

These are proven largemouth bass lures, and pike and muskie love them, too. Often called "spinnerbaits" or "buzz baits," they work well when retrieved over weeds, with pauses to let them flutter into holes or along edges. Their design makes them almost snag-proof, so they are a good bet when working cover for aggressive fish.

Another variation of the safety-pin spinner is the Beetle Spin and its clones. Often smaller than the spinnerbaits described above, they have a single blade on the upper arm and a jig and grub attached to the lower arm instead of the skirted, weighted head.

I like the versatility of these lures, primarily because I can easily change the jig and grub, which alters the color and overall look considerably. They can be fished as described above or even trolled. They work very well at slow speeds, too. Their smaller, more innocuous look makes them a good bet for skittish fish or for fishing after a cold front.

Combos, Oddballs, and Critters
▶ *Favorite floating jig colors: black, red, white, yellow, chartreuse*
▶ *Species: walleye, bass, panfish*

▶ *Favorite safety-pin spinner colors: silver, black, brass, white, chartreuse*
▶ *Species: pike, bass, muskie, walleye*

▶ *Favorite plastic worm and critter colors: black, blue, purple, smoke, natural, shad, crawdad*
▶ *Species: bass, walleye*

Many soft plastic baits, such as most of the grubs, are designed to be used in conjunction with another lure, like a jig. But some, like 4- to 8-inch worms and "critters" (salamanders, crayfish, or frog imitators), are used alone.

With specialized "worm" hooks and cone-shaped sinkers, plastic worms can be rigged to be weedless. The point of the hook is buried within the body of the bait, allowing it to be fished in the thickest cover, which makes this setup

Spinnerbaits (left and top right) are versatile lures that are great for working over, around, and through weeds. Critters (bottom right) are designed to be used on their own, and smaller ones can be attached to jig heads, as well.

a great choice for largemouth. Rigged this way, you need a powerful hook-set to connect with the fish, so beef up your tackle. You'll need a stiff rod and at least 14-pound line to hook and haul hawgs out of heavy cover.

I've also had good success with walleye and smallmouth using some of the smaller critters on a jig. The plastics used today, especially some of the scented ones, have almost eliminated the need for live bait in many situations. They are so lifelike that many fish hang on to them for several seconds and sometimes even swallow them.

CHAPTER 4

Honest—I Didn't Fib!

At this point, some of you may be thinking: "Frank, you're a big fat liar! At the beginning of this book, which, by the way, I am starting to regret buying, you said, and I quote, 'There are only two ways to catch a fish.' And here you've blathered on for page after page about trolling, casting, still-fishing, using live bait, spinners, and plugs, fishing streams, rivers, and lakes, and yadda-yadda-yadda."

Whoa.

Easy, big guy.

I'm innocent. Really. There *are* only two ways to catch a fish.

▶ **You can either entice them or you can provoke them.**

Whether you are using live or artificial bait, trolling or casting, fishing fast or slow, you are trying to coerce a fish into striking either by *fooling them* or by *triggering a reactive attack.*

All presentations are designed to do one or the other. In fact, sometimes doing one accomplishes the other.

Fly-fishing purists may wince, but just like the angler artfully working a popper or the kid drowning a worm, they are trying to entice a fish into taking what they are offering.

Enticing fish means giving them exactly what they want in the form of bait or finessing them into believing that your fly is just like the ones they are rising for or that the popper you're retrieving is really an injured frog.

There is a definite element of deception in enticing fish (covered in chapters 2 and 3).

Provoking a strike can be divided into two categories (so you nitpickers out there can just sue me!). There's the instinctive or reactive strike and the angry one.

The Reactive or Instinctive Strike

You've just enjoyed a wonderful meal. You're pretty darn full and are contemplating whether or not to undo the top button on your pants when out of the kitchen comes Grandma. And the dear, sweet woman is bearing a fresh-from-the-oven apple pie!

You're really not hungry, but it looks and smells so good! If you were alone, you might pass and have some later. But there are seven other people at the table, and you notice most of them are drooling. You sigh, undo the button, and have a slice.

Now, you're a 3-pound walleye just returning from a successful foray to a nearby weed bed. Two yearling perch are digesting nicely in your belly. You and the rest of your school are scattered along a wide break, this month's home.

Something's coming. Looks like an injured minnow. You're really not hungry . . . but maybe the next trip to the weed bed won't be so rewarding. It's getting closer and you can see and sense a few of your brothers and sisters stirring . . . showing an interest in that rapidly approaching minnow . . . *your* minnow!

The Angry Strike

This time, you're curled up at home reading a good book. Maybe even a *really* good book—like this one. A fly buzzes past. You ignore it. It zips past your nose this time, and you glare at it.

Fishing Hail Marys

I was raised a Catholic in the 1950s. In those days, life was pretty much a minefield of sin. You had to tread carefully. As a general rule, if something was enjoyable, it was wrong. Deception fell squarely under the umbrella of Lying, a definite sin.

Hmmmm . . . fishing = fun . . . deception = bad . . . how to reconcile? Luckily, a heartfelt apology would absolve most minor sins. Now I murmur a "sorry, buddy" as I unhook a fish. Works for me.

Now the darn thing is hovering around your head and buzzing like a chain saw. Two minutes ago you were unaware of that fly's existence.

Now you're going to end it.

You're a 30-pound chinook salmon headed upstream to spawn. You're not hungry. In fact, you can't eat because your throat is constricted, part of a pre-spawn physiological response.

Something flashy is buzzing toward you. You shift aside, letting it pass.

It comes again, you shift again. Again. And yet again.

Next time you decide to kill it.

If you're fishing, you are either a seducer, a troublemaker, or both. You are a combination of Don Juan and Dennis the Menace.

I believe the walleye scenario above, the reactive strike with an element of enticement, accounts for most of the fish that are hooked. It illustrates the opportunistic nature of fish, indeed of all wildlife, including us. Who among us wouldn't bend to pick up a $5 bill the breeze happens to blow our way?

▶ **Fish are not actively feeding much of the time. They are usually in a neutral or negative mood. But fish are opportunistic most of the time and ornery some of the time. A neutral fish will rarely pass up an easy meal, and even a negative fish can get ticked off.**

Well then, if all fish can either be teased or provoked into striking, how come we still get skunked sometimes?

Ah, now we finally arrive at that aspect of fishing at which we can all excel: Making Excuses.

The guy at the bait shop lied . . . it's too hot-cold-sunny-windy . . . it's not hot-cold-sunny-windy *enough* . . . there *are* no fish in this lake . . . they were hitting Day-Glo Tie-Dyed Dollar Stealers and I only had the iridescent ones . . . and did I mention that the bait-shop guy lied?

▶ **Christ adopted a group of fishermen to be his disciples. Every now and then, to appease whining golfers, who were completely overlooked, we have to get skunked.**

Everybody gets skunked once in a while. But if you get skunked a lot, you're doing something, probably several somethings, wrong. (Or,

NOT-SO-TALL TALE

In the Company of Carp

Attending college and working full-time during the summers didn't leave me with a lot of fishing time. I missed it, though, and would often pause while crossing a bridge over the river that ran through my campus to gaze longingly at the water.

I graduated, but my wife-to-be still had a year of school to go, so I found a job on campus to stay close by. One day while river watching I spotted three or four largish shadows below me. I realized they were carp.

The next morning, on my day off, I was trundling along the bank with my rod in one hand and a loaf of fresh bread in the other. I found a likely looking pool, squeezed some bread into a ball around my hook, and tossed it in. A few minutes later I was engaged in a spirited tug of war with a plucky 5-pound carp.

It would be the first of many pleasant mornings. A 24-hour coffee shop was located along my route. I would grab the morning paper, a coffee, and a couple doughnuts, and walk down to my favorite pool. By sunrise I would be sharing my bread and doughnuts with the carp, who provided me with a lot of fun in return. Between engagements I would read the paper and sip my coffee. None of the carp were huge—2 to 12 pounds—and I released them all. I'm sure I caught the same fish many times over during the course of those months. I'm beholden to those homely critters for keeping me connected to a pastime I loved, and with which I'd been in danger of losing touch.

The next decade brought marriage, a return to our hometown, a job in a tackle shop, and my first articles about fishing in newspapers and magazines. I fished every chance I got. ◄◄

maybe there really *are* no fish in that lake.)

▶ **Fishless days usually happen for one of two reasons. You may not have been "on" the fish: you were fishing where they were not. Or, you were on them, but something about your presentation—speed, size, smell, weight—wasn't right.**

But you read this book (at least up to this point). You did your homework. You did everything right. And you still didn't catch a thing.

Well, there's yet another reason for skunkings.

Two words that can make the seasoned pro turn pale. The excuse that is no longer an excuse because it has been elevated into a Reason.

You, my fishless friend, have been the victim of a Cold Front.

Which brings us to . . .

CHAPTER 5

When to Fish

One of the first things a novice wants to know is, "When is the best time to go fishing?"

The correct answer, of course, is the same as it is for most of life's Great Questions: It depends.

My general rule of thumb for when to fish is pretty basic: if there is no lightning, I'm out there. (Lightning is a fine series of rods made by Berkley. This is a good example of how the name of something does not necessarily indicate its designated purpose.)

Another common and correct answer is, "Go whenever you can." You're not likely to catch any fish while parked on your sofa, so get out on the water.

But let me try to narrow it down.

Dawn and dusk are classic "good" times. Another good time is after a rain has raised and stained—but not flooded and muddied—a stream or river. Cloudy, breezy days are better than still, clear days. Periods of stable weather and before, *not* during, a storm are good times. I also like fishing during rains (again, *not* storms). Fishing at night can be excellent for many species, especially on bodies of water that see a lot of fishing pressure or daytime boat traffic. (Walleye are the classic example of this.)

But "when" to go fishing is based on more than just the daily conditions or time of day, it can mean the season. Fish move, particularly on large bodies of water. Spawning fish aren't where they were one, three, or six months earlier, and they behave differently. Seasonal changes alter a fish's metabolism and often change its location and feeding patterns.

Muskie anglers are well aware that in the fall muskies seek to pack on the pounds to carry them through the slim pickings of winter. So anglers use oversized lures to tempt them.

For a week or so every summer, the walleye on my home lake gorge themselves on emerging mayflies. The perch can relax for a while, as the walleye are on the mud flats.

Because fish are cold blooded, their internal thermostats reflect the temperature of their environment. Generally speaking, when it's cold, they are sluggish. When it's warm, they're more active. (And, yes, I know there are exceptions to this. Rules are no darn good without exceptions.) A

NOT-SO-TALL TALE

Good Things Come . . .

My fishing buddy Phil once taught me a valuable lesson about patience.

We were working a stream for browns and hadn't gone too far from the car when we came upon a beautiful pool, much larger than most in that small stream and nearly deep enough to swim in. Phil began to fish it, and I moved on upstream. I had covered about a half-mile of water, fishing through more than a dozen smallish holes in well over an hour, without Phil catching up with me. I doubled back, fishing some of the holes again. Two hours had passed by the time I got back to that nice pool where I'd left Phil, and I'd caught a couple of decent 12-inch browns during my travels.

Phil had made himself comfortable. His rod was resting on a forked stick, and he was leaning back against the bank, hands folded behind his head, cap tilted over his eyes, half-asleep. I was about to razz him when I saw a pair of beautiful browns lying beside him in the shade, about 15 and 17 inches respectively.

He explained that in the first half-hour, all he'd caught were a few chub and a sucker. Then he got the 15-incher. Another hour passed during which time he got another couple of suckers. Then the 17-incher hit.

I was sweat-soaked, scratched from brush and branches, and had a couple of middling-sized trout. He hadn't budged, out-fishing me while working on his tan. If I had fished that hole alone, at that stage of my fishing life, I would have moved on after ten minutes or after the third chub or sucker. I wouldn't have caught those trout.

Thanks to Phil, I learned that sometimes when you are fishing on great water you just have to out-wait the fish. ◄◄◄

quick-moving lure will generate more interest in summer than spring.

> ▶ **So, the "When" to fish will lead you to the "Where" and the "How."**

And you thought it was going to be *so* simple.

Nighttime Can Be the Right Time

Many anglers develop tans from days spent on the water. A few, however, have the pasty pallor of vampires. We call these creatures "night fishermen." They know and practice stuff that most of us don't. They know that it's not just huge walleye with eyes like onions that feed at night. They catch bass, trout, salmon, and catfish too, long after the sun is down.

Remember the fish's basic requirements of safety, protection, and cover? Well, night is the ultimate cover.

While eagles, osprey, gulls—and most of us—are catching a few winks, a lot of fish are hunting for a midnight snack. And a few anglers are hunting for them.

The biggest advantage to night fishing is that you often have the whole playing field to yourself.

My brother Karl with a nice walleye. Further proof that nighttime can be the right time.

The biggest disadvantage is that you can't *see* the darn playing field!

Inexperienced boaters and anglers should never fish alone at night. This is a recipe for disaster.

But if you're sane, sober, and experienced, night fishing can be a delight.

Some seasoned night owls swear that the darkest moonless nights are best. As for me, I don't want to catch a fish *that* bad. *Some* light from the stars and moon makes night fishing easier and less dangerous.

Once your eyes adjust, a clear, starry night with some moonlight allows you to spot marker buoys *before* you feel that sickening thud and remember, "Oh, yeah, *that* shoal."

All your other senses are heightened at night. A loon's cry is more mournful. You can smell the wood smoke from dying campfires. Every fish feels bigger and seems to fight harder than the ones you catch during the day. As an added bonus, the ones that get away can be as big as your imagination allows!

Full moon nights are magical on the water. The moon's ghostly glow illuminates a world so hauntingly beautiful it can take your breath away. Often, it is bright enough to land fish without a light, and sometimes you can even retie lures by moonlight.

But if you are ill-prepared, night fishing can be a nightmare. Not many people know this, but Murphy's Law was developed and then perfected by a night fisherman.

Wear your life jacket.

Don't bring any unessential tackle boxes, and de-clutter your boat of other extraneous gear. Like the owl, "extra stuff" is active at night and will attempt to trip you just as you're about to net a 10-pound walleye (whereupon you'll be darn glad you wore your life jacket).

Rig your rods before you hit the water. The less you use your flashlight, the more readily your eyes will adjust, and readjust, to the available light, so have your tackle ready to go.

I like to use minnow-type plugs fished at least 3 feet above bottom. Even higher is OK. Fish will be looking up and to the sides for prey, and they'll spot it silhouetted against the surface.

If you're fishing from a boat, make sure it has running lights. If it doesn't, invest in one of those 6-volt lanterns with a small flashing red or orange light, and keep the flasher *on*. You might not be the only angler out there. You'll want to know where they are, and they'll want to be able to keep tabs on you, too.

Bring a small flashlight (with an adjustable beam) that you can hold in your mouth. Have another larger one, or that lantern, for backup and for spotlighting your way when under power. It's a proven scientific fact that 91 percent of all floating logs appear only at night. It helps to see them before they greet you.

If you're trolling with an outboard, let out two or three times as much line as usual. Generally, the fish are shallower, and therefore spookier, than during the day. A long lead lets them regroup after scattering from the noise and before your lure dances by.

I used to fish at night quite a bit in the years B.C. (Before Children). In those days I would regularly pull an all-nighter, fueled by youth, coffee, and a handful of antacids.

Minnow imitators, shallow-to-medium running cranks, and jerks are best for night fishing.

When It Rains . . .

As I mentioned earlier, I also like to fish while it's raining. Cold, dark, rainy days leave the Others downcast, but they lift an angler's heart.

Rain and wind wash food into streams, stain the water, and coax fish out of deep cover. On lakes, rain cuts light penetration so fish become more comfortable visiting shallower feeding areas during daylight hours. "Dirty" weather often precedes a cold front, so fish go on a feeding binge.

▶ **Fish are always more "catchable" in inclement weather.**

An example: The headwaters of my home creek are small, brushy, cold, and, normally, as clear as gin. There are few good pools, but a lot of undercut banks and deadfall. The water is home to both native brown and brook trout, averaging 9 to 16 inches. On a typical outing, using a stealthy approach and a delicate presentation, I might catch four or five trout. The stretch I usual fish includes about a mile of water.

One overcast day, I neared my usual "turning back" point having done reasonably well, about three or four fish. Then the skies opened, and the rain came down with a vengeance. As I began to work my way back toward the car, the water rose and became discolored. On the same stretch of water I had just fished, I caught nearly thirty more trout. On a normal day, I may have gotten one or two more.

▶ **Fish lose their caution during periods when water is rising and discolored.**

The fish had abandoned their hidey-holes and were sitting in the main current, gorging on the bounty washing past and safe from sharp-eyed predators. Fishing *after* a rain, when the water is still discolored but dropping can also be good, especially for migratory fish, which are often waiting for a fresh rain to kick off their run upriver. But resident fish are often gorged to the gills by that time. For them, nothing beats that period when the water is rising.

Well, I guess I've stalled long enough.

Cold Fronts

You have a three-day fishing weekend planned. You've been rearranging your tackle and daydreaming of lunkers for weeks. The weather has been warm and stable for ten days. The last two days before you leave have been a little hot and sticky. It will be nice to be on the water.

The evening you arrive at your fishing destination is punctuated by a series of thunderstorms. Your spouse is relieved, the humidity will be broken.

You are stricken. And daylight confirms your deepest fears, bright blue sky, dry air, and a brisk northeast wind.

The Others call this a beautiful day.

We call it a cold front. If you want to sound like a grizzled veteran, even if you've never punctured any part of your anatomy with a treble hook, drop the "cold" and just call it a "front," or refer to it by its proper, scientific name, "damned front."

Old-timers had plenty of theories about why fronts shut down the fishing. The fish had gotten lockjaw. The weather change caused them to lose their teeth. They all died.

The commonly accepted theory today is that the change in temperature, though often relatively slight, is enough to affect fish metabolism. It slows them down for a few days until they adjust to it or the temperature returns to previous levels.

I think this is only partly true. The main reason they don't hit with gusto is simpler.

They're full. Stuffed. Gorged. Sated. They've undone the top button of their pants.

Every time we hop a jig or wiggle a lure past their noses, they belch delicately behind their napkins and murmur, "Oh, dear, no thank you. Couldn't possibly. Really. Perhaps another time."

Fish don't need a weather channel. They know well in advance, probably by the change in barometric pressure, that a front is on the way. They know from experience they'll soon be feeling sluggish for a day—or three.

And so will their prey. Holding tight to cover. Harder to find. More trouble than it's worth.

Their solution is simple and pragmatic.

Front coming. *Eat Now. Eat MUCH Now!*

If you've been lucky enough to be "on" fish in advance of a storm, when the wind freshens and dark cumulus clouds seem to graze the treetops, you've probably experienced some memorable fishing. Fish often hit with a reckless abandon until the lightning starts. They may continue feeding after that, but I've never stayed to find out.

I've experienced this action many times, but it's a little like playing Russian roulette. You *must* know how long it will take you to get back to safety. You *must* be realistic about your boat-handling skills and your boat's capabilities in rough water. If you're uncertain about any of the above, then get off the water at the first rumble of thunder, sooner if you're a long way from shelter.

Your life isn't worth a 5-pound walleye. Arguably, it *might* not even be worth an 8- or 10-pounder. Best to err on the side of caution.

OK, knowing about this predictable feeding frenzy is all well and good. But you missed it. The front has moved in. Knowing why the fish aren't going to hit isn't doing a thing for your confidence. You still have three days of fishing ahead of you.

There's hope. Fronts make fishing tougher, but not impossible.

Remember the walleye that ate the two perch and then let peer pressure and opportunism push it into swiping at your plug? Well, it's time to refine that approach.

▶ **Think of the three S's when dealing with a front: small, slow, and still.**

The fish haven't disappeared, and they do still have their teeth. However, they are unlikely to be found in feeding areas or along routes to and from feeding areas. They are at home, resting and digesting.

If you use small lures or bait, fished *very* slowly, you can tempt a few of them to hit.

I will back-troll, or drift if the wind is slight, with a small floating jig head tipped with part of a worm. Or I'll use a floating-worm rig with a small or half worm. This approach has saved my bacon during many a front.

▶ **If you usually use 8-pound line or heavier, now is a good time to drop down to 6- or even 4-pound. You don't have to change your whole spool. Somewhere in one of your pockets or tackle boxes is a spool of lighter line and some barrel swivels. Find them, I'll wait.**

OK. Put your main line through your egg sinker and tie it to one end of the barrel swivel. Now the swivel plays the part that your split shot used to: it stops the egg sinker from sliding down to your hook.

Cut 2 to 3 feet of line off your lighter spool. Attach your hook to one end and tie the other to the other end of the barrel swivel. Presto! You now have a 4- or 6-pound leader!

There are a lot of situations where a lighter leader can make the difference between a fish-less and fish-full day.

Usually, however, a front brings fairly brisk winds, making water conditions too fast for drifting. And sometimes even a back-troll or trolling with an electric motor is too fast. First, try trolling *into* the wind. Sometimes it's just the ticket. Other times, it makes boat control too difficult. If so, what now?

Don't fret, cold fronts are why God made anchors.

This is where the third S comes in—*still.*

Anchor within casting range of where you know, or suspect, or hope, the fish are. You can cast the same rig with which you were just back-trolling, but you'll do better if you refine it a little more.

▶ **The slower your presentation, the more subtle your offering must appear.**

My all-round sinker of choice is a $1/2$-ounce egg or walking-type sinker. In shallow water or at slow speeds, I'll switch to a $1/4$-ounce. While anchored during a front, however, I'll usually go to either a $1/8$-ounce egg or simply use a small split shot to weight my offering. You'll lose distance on your casts, so anchor closer to your target area.

I'll also shorten my lead, the distance from sinker to hook, to about 8 or 10 inches. These fish are hunkered down! They're like you after Thanksgiving dinner. They are on the couch and can barely operate the remote, let alone move 2 or 3 feet to eat anything.

The lighter weight also makes for a more natural presentation. A $1/2$- to $1/4$-ounce sinker plummets like a stone and lands with a perceptible (and spooky) thud. A little snack that wafts gently down to wriggle helplessly in front of Mr. Fish's nose is much more appealing.

I usually use a floating worm or half-worm when still-fishing. A floating jig head has to be retrieved to be effective. A worm can just sit there. Every 30 seconds or so, I'll bring it toward the boat a foot or two and then pause again. This is much more effective during a cold front than a steady retrieve.

Using a float to present live bait is also a front-friendly tactic. Your minnow, worm, or leech *must* be very close to bottom, though, so you may have to rig up a slip float and do a little testing until you're sure you're within a foot or two of bottom (see slip float on page 38).

I don't fear fronts the way I used to. Now I almost welcome the chance

More Cold Front Dos and Don'ts

1 Fronts don't seem to have the same deleterious effect on moving water. Perhaps it's because the heavy rain often causes ■ roily, fast water that makes foraging difficult. The fish feed, often in a frenzy, while the water is rising, stop when it's at its height, and resume as it clears.

2. Fronts demand patience. Anglers are famous for exhibiting patience. The Others often mistake our ox-like imperturbability for stupidity. It's not. We're not. We're just really, really . . . um . . . patient.

3. If your target species is holding tight to cover, like a weed bed, forget spinnerbaits. If the water is calm, as it often is in back bays, try small poppers. Or dunk jigs as slowly as possible. Use a flattened, wedge-shaped head that sinks slowly. You can also try using bait under a float in the nearest open area. A fish's opportunism often overcomes its inertia if you're patient enough. That's patient, not stupid.

4. If you're a fidgeter and the Do-Nothing approach drives you crazy, either take a Valium and get over it or try twitching (not hopping) a small jig with a scented body or tipped with bait. Or go do something else, like fix that darn leaky toilet you've been meaning to get to.

Sometimes you're going to do everything right and still get skunked. So what? Sometimes the home team loses. You got some fresh air and a healthy dose of peace and quiet. Who's going to call that a bad day?

to slow down and get back to basics. Once your bait is where you want it, you can open your bail and set the rod down. This hands-free fishing gives you a chance to look around and enjoy the scenery. Eat a snack. Scratch that itch. Apply more sunscreen.

You can watch the fishin' technicians race from spot to spot, eyes glued to their sonars, trying to distinguish those low-lying fish from bottom debris. You can wave to them cheerfully as their wakes rock your boat. You've got a nice walleye and smallmouth in your cooler. You've released three others and . . . where the heck did that float go? It was just there a second ago . . .

Know what?

The Others were right, it *is* a beautiful day!

CHAPTER **6**

Gear and Tackle

If you're an avid fisherman, chances are you'll already have built an addition to your house or rented a storage unit to accommodate your accumulation of gear.

But for the neophyte or occasional angler, the following information is divided between what you *need* to have and what you'll *want* to get.

Having managed to survive for 51 years without ever making a decent wage, I'll naturally try to make this easy for the budget-conscious. In fact, it's entirely possible to get reasonably outfitted for less than a house down payment!

Gotta Have It

I've already talked about the rod and reel (see page 29). If a spare spool is available for your reel, get one. You can fill one with 8-pound test, the other with lighter or heavier monofilament depending on where you're going to fish, and for what.

You'll need an assortment of sinkers, both egg and split shot. Hooks are right up there in the "necessary" department. Tailor them to your quarry, but make sure you've got some short-shanked, wide gap (but not *too* wide) #8 and #10 hooks. For panfishing with kids, the longer shank and narrower gap of Carlisle and Kirby hooks make hook removal easier.

Don't buy cheap hooks. Avoid the poly-bagged, no-name variety offering 15 or 20 hooks for 99 cents. Very good hooks will cost $3 to $5 for a pack of 25. About $5 will buy you 50 reasonably good hooks. Good hooks are sticky-sharp right out of the package and will hold their edge longer than cheap ones. If you're only going to get a couple of bites in a day, you'll be happy you spent the few extra pennies when you hook and hold those few fish.

Now invest in a few pencil floats, say two each of the three most popular sizes. Might as well get a worm blower, too. Don't forget long-nosed pliers or forceps. A fillet knife will come in handy if you plan to eat some of your catch. Depending on where you're fishing and what species you are chasing, you might need a net. The shallow-bagged rubber nets are easier on fish,

Gear Essentials

- 6½- to 7-foot medium-action spinning rod with light- to medium-sized reel spooled with 8-pound test line
- selection of quality hooks
- a variety of sinkers
- at least six floats of your choice in three sizes
- worm blower
- needle-nose pliers
- nail clippers
- fillet knife
- bait and (possibly) net
- a watery destination full of finned critters that you can share this stuff with

but the large ones are quite heavy and difficult for a solo angler to use. Find one that best suits your current needs. Oh, and buy a set of nail clippers so you don't chip a tooth from years of line-biting, like that guy in the mirror.

Guess what?

With what you've got so far, all you need is some bait and you're ready to catch trout, bass, walleye, catfish, carp, and panfish.

Yes, it's true! You can stop right there and be reasonably successful catching a wide variety of fish.

But . . .

If you want to be a little more versatile in your presentation, if you're pretty sure this fishing thing isn't just a passing fancy, if you've got the bug and got it bad . . . you'll *need* more stuff.

Gotta Have It for Moving Water

If you intend to fish streams or rivers, you'll need decent waders. If the water depth is greater than 3 feet you'll need chest waders, although booted hip waders will suffice for most situations. In either case, you don't need the best

Essential Gear for Moving Water

In addition to the basics outlined in the Gear Essentials sidebar on page 73 you'll need:

- waders with felt insoles
- an assortment of snap swivels, and lures, and boxes to hold them
- sunglasses, hat, sunscreen, and insect repellent
- extra line
- a too-big vest to hold this collection of goodies

quality waders right off the bat. If you intend to fish in cold water, get insulated boots. Most waders come with a felt insole. If they don't, make sure the store sells insoles that can be placed inside before you try them on. (You'll thank me for this later.) Wear a heavy pair of socks. Some boots also come with felt or other nonslip bottoms for surer purchase on slippery rocks. The waters you intend to fish will dictate whether these are necessary.

You'll need at least a modest selection of spinners and plugs. If your river hosts bass, pike, muskie, or walleye, you'll also need jigs. You'll want some barrel- and ball-bearing snap swivels and a few split rings. To hold all these goodies, you'll need one or two or five small boxes that are large enough to hold your selection but small enough to fit in a pocket. Pack extra line, just in case, and don't forget bug repellent, sunscreen, hat, and sunglasses.

Hey, this stuff is making quite a pile! How are you going to carry it all as you plod up and down the river?

Ladies and gentlemen, may I present to you the third most important piece of equipment (after the rod and reel): The Vest!

The vest was yet another brilliant idea born of necessity. Somebody handy with a needle and thread got fed up with trudging back to shore to rummage around in a bag or tackle box every time he or she needed to change a lure or add some weight.

Voilà!

Now we have a vest with 97 pockets to hold every conceivable doodad, gadget, whatsis, and thingamabob. And it leaves your hands free for fishing! It has put an end to that sinking realization that you forgot your tackle box four holes back.

When shopping for a vest, there is only one criterion: pockets. I mentioned early in the book that there are few absolute rules in the world of angling. Here comes one.

▶ ****A vest cannot have too many pockets.****

Carefully assess the front of your potential purchase. This is where you'll be stashing the stuff you want most readily accessible. Are there more than 2 square inches of fabric without a pocket, either handy or hidden? If so, forget it—too much wasted space.

If it passes the initial pocket scrutiny, do these pockets come in a variety of sizes with different types of closures? Some should be zippered, some flapped. Some should be wide and deep enough for big stuff, others small enough that you can barely get your fingers in for the tiny stuff. Most should fall in between, for the bulk of your stuff. Does the vest have a fluffy, white hook-keeper on the upper left side?

If your vest survived these initial tests, you may now try it on.

Make sure the vest is big enough to fit over whatever you might conceivably wear. I'm not particularly big, but my vest is 2XX Large. I fish for trout and salmon in *very* cold weather, and my vest has to fit over several layers of clothing. Of course, in T-shirt weather, I look like a kid wearing his dad's vest, but no fish I've ever caught commented on my lack of fashion sense.

While wearing it, open the sides to look at the inside panels. Lots of pockets? At least two on each side that took you a while to find? Nice tight, Velcro closures that are practically impossible to open one-handed?

If you can answer "yes" to all these questions, *and* if the vest is *much* too big for you, buy it.

▶ **You'll know you've got a real gem if after you've been wearing your vest for a year or more you discover a pocket you had no idea was there. If you're like me, you'll immediately fill it with some-**

MAGIC PORTRAITS

The Author demonstrates that even a too-large vest with 97 pockets has *some* limitations.

thing perishable, like roe bags, then promptly forget about it again until the contents must be removed with the help of forceps and an oxygen mask.

A good vest is invaluable. It gives us our freedom. Unfortunately, it also, at least eventually, gives us slumped shoulders and sore necks. But hey! That's down the road. Right now, with what I've described above, your vest probably weighs less than 10 pounds. You're ready, tiger! Go get 'em!

Gotta Have It for the Boat Angler

For fishing from a boat, you'll need all of the above—except the waders—plus a few other things.

First among them is a tackle box. Tackle boxes are for holding gear that's too big or too dangerous to keep in your vest. You *don't* want to fumble around in a vest pocket for a lure with three sets of treble hooks. (OK, maybe once, just to see what it's like.) Tackle boxes come in a variety of designs and sizes, from lunch bag to suitcase. Let's pretend that you only need one (insert stifled laughter here).

I would recommend the reversible, satchel-style box with dividers that can be manipulated to alter the size of the trays. On one side, you can put your spinners, plugs, and spoons. On the other, your hooks, sinkers, jigs, and plastics.

A traditional tackle box with three or four trays and a storage "belly" would also do the job. The belly of these boxes is usually big enough to hold extra spools of line or other bulky items.

I always take a fairly large cooler with me in the boat. I use it to keep my bait fresh and to store fish I intend to keep and eat. The top of the cooler is also a handy perch for my tackle box(es) when I need to peruse the contents in search of inspiration.

On big water, a floating marker buoy is handy when you get a good fish and want to mark the spot. Unfortunately, you'll also be announcing your success to every passing boater.

Make sure your boat has an anchor with a sufficient length of rope.

Essential Gear for the Boat Angler

Everything previously mentioned plus:
- a tackle box (or four)
- a cooler
- a floating marker buoy
- anchor with sufficient rope
- compass
- map or chart
- CB or VHF radio for larger waters
- electric trolling motor for larger craft

(Remember the third S for dealing with a cold front.) An anchor can also prevent you from running aground if you develop motor trouble. (By the way, I'm assuming your boat has the requisite safety equipment mandated by your jurisdiction.)

A compass, chart, and a VHF or CB radio are necessities if you intend to fish large bodies of water such as the Great Lakes. The compass and chart help you only if you have some working knowledge of navigation. If you don't know basic navigation, either take a class and read some books, or just stay off these larger bodies of water. Or stay in sight of shore. The radio informs you of weather changes, lets you swap info with other anglers, and lets you call for help if the need arises.

If your boat is powered by a motor of 25 horsepower or more, the addition of an electric trolling motor moves from optional to nearly essential. There are times when you must move slowly to fish properly. An electric motor gives you that option in almost any situation.

What You Want

The title of this section is a bit of misnomer because what you *want* inevitably evolves into what you convince yourself you *need*.

As a general rule, it means *more* of everything.

There are strange and powerful forces at work here, some perfectly reasonable, others arcane and mysterious.

It makes perfect sense that if you fish for a variety of species—some measured in ounces, some over 30 pounds—in a variety of water conditions, you'll need a wider selection of rods, reels, hooks, and lures. You'll also need more and bigger containers to hold this expanding collection.

It's physics, really, and the law, a variant of the Vest Law, is immutable:

▶ **No matter how large a tackle box, no matter how many pockets in a vest, they are neither large nor plentiful enough to hold the entire stock of a tackle shop.**

And that, of course, is exactly what the avid angler aspires to own, a tackle shop—only portable.

As to the more mysterious reasons for this phenomenon, well, remember the look on your child's face on Christmas morning? Or maybe the first time he or she went to Toys Я Us? Maybe *you* were that child, eyes huge with wonder, gasping at the sheer magnitude of . . . all . . . that . . . stuff.

Well, something similar happens when you become a true fisherman.

My theory is that the fresh air and hot sun, combined with laser-focused concentration, hour after hour, day after day, has a cumulative effect over the years. Seasoned anglers develop a near Zenlike state akin to that of an enlightened sage or a delighted, innocent child. Our senses become permanently *heightened.* We see the world with new eyes, despite our advancing years.

Nowhere does this childlike wonder become more apparent than when we step into a tackle shop. Here's an example.

Let's say a novice angler and I are entering a tackle shop at the same time. We both came because we are low on #5 split shot, costing about a dollar a package.

We enter the shop together. He goes directly to the sinker display, selects two packages, and heads to the cash register. He pays for the purchase and walks to the door.

He has to step around me because I am still rooted just inside the entrance, gazing raptly at all the displays . . . the colors . . . the shapes. As he leaves, the door chimes snap my reverie, and I head to the sinker section.

To get there, however, I have to pass the spinners. My Heightened Awareness is fully activated now, so I'm able to tell at a glance that in the Blue Fox section there are two new colors!

They are bright and shiny.

My feet stop moving and my hand reaches out. Seconds later, I have one of each new color in three different sizes.

Say, what's that at the end of the aisle? Ohmigod! It's a clearance bin! And it's full! I hurry over. My eyes light up at the sign, "Your Choice: $2 each or 6 for $10."

I slowly do the math. (Strangely, Heightened Awareness actually seems to diminish certain other brain functions.) The bin is full of blister-packed plugs and spoons that probably only caught fish in the designer's dreams. No matter.

They are bright and shiny.

I buy 12.

My arms are full, so I take my goodies to the counter to set them down before fetching my sinkers. The man behind the counter is opening a small box. It contains an ultralight spinning reel. He glances at me and says casually, "New one from Abu Garcia."

I am not looking at him.

The reel is bright and shiny.

And a bargain at only $69.99. The man is very nice. He tells me that they have a new 6-foot light-action boron-graphite rod that's a perfect mate to this reel. If I buy both, he can give me 15 percent off.

I don't need to do the math. Fifteen percent is a lot!

Such a nice man. I hurry to the rod racks.

Thirty minutes later, I leave the store, beaming and laden with purchases.

Back home, opening and sorting, arranging and rearranging, my happiness dims slightly when I realize I have forgotten the sinkers.

If only all problems were so easily remedied. I'll just have to go back tomorrow.

The Others, of course, cannot grasp the concept of Heightened Awareness. The few I have tried explaining it to have called me gullible, even referred to me as being that word that begins with an S. One even muttered something completely nonsensical about mad dogs and English fishermen.

I have little doubt that they are equally poor at understanding physics.

But I digressed a little there.

Besides a greater quantity and a wider variety of everything, there is one other piece of gear that eventually becomes essential.

▶ **If you become more than a casual angler, you will need good-quality foul-weather clothing.**

Years ago, I would go fishing on dirty days in a traditional rubber or vinyl raincoat or poncho. Within an hour or two I would be wet inside and out, miserable and nearly hypothermic, even if the temperature was in the 50s (Fahrenheit).

Now I am often out in weather in the 40-degree range or lower, in wind-whipped driving rain or sleet that feels like ice needles. And I catch fish. And I'm reasonably comfortable.

The difference, of course, is the clothing. New rain gear is breathable; moisture evaporates from the inside, even if water eventually permeates the outer shell. You don't get "clammy" on the inside, and you retain heat better.

Quality foul-weather clothing is expensive, but worth every penny. It is available insulated or noninsulated. I prefer a three-quarter-length parka-style, noninsulated coat with a hood.

Insulated coats are too hot for rain during warmer weather. If you buy a roomy, noninsulated coat, you can wear layers underneath on cold days or a T-shirt on warm ones. Make sure it has lots of pockets that have tight closures. The wrists should have well-made elastic cuffs or adjustable Velcro closures. The hood is great for when the wind is driving the rain or snow from behind you. You can lose a lot of heat from the nape of your neck.

If you mostly fish moving water, waders are sufficient for your lower body. You might get the chest-style for more complete protection. These also let you sit on muddy banks while keeping your drawers dry.

If you fish from a boat, pier, or other stationary area, invest in good rain pants, as well. Again, make sure they're roomy enough to pull on over your regular pants. Pockets should be zippered, and the area from calf to ankle should be adjustable to make them easier to remove over boots. Guys, make sure there's a fly.

A wide-brimmed hat keeps the rain off your face and your head and neck dry. If very cold, wear a brimmed cap with earflaps and use the hood of your coat. Don't neglect your hands: wool fingerless gloves retain some warmth, even when wet, and keep your fingertips free for tying hooks, etc. (if they're not numb as posts).

Hypothermia is a very real danger, and if you're stationary, as many anglers are, it can occur at surprisingly high temperatures.

But saving your life is just a bonus for investing in quality foul-weather clothing. The real payoff comes when you are warm, dry, and catching fish in weather that sends the unprepared back to their cars or keeps them at home.

What You Want for Your Boat

If you invest in a fishing boat, it's only a matter of time before you consider buying expensive gear, mostly electronics.

If you fish for suspended fish in big water, like Great Lakes salmon, your job will be easier with downriggers, a graph, and a temperature probe.

A downrigger is a device like a giant reel that holds 200 feet of wire, with a 2- to 4-foot rod that mounts securely to the side or stern of the boat. At the end of the wire you attach a heavy lead weight, called a "cannonball," that weighs about 8 pounds. Attached to the ball is a clip to which you attach your line. The main purpose of a rigger is to allow you to fish in very deep water with

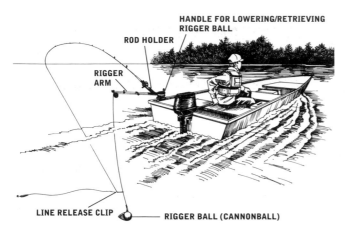

HANDLE FOR LOWERING/RETRIEVING
RIGGER BALL

ROD HOLDER

RIGGER
ARM

LINE RELEASE CLIP   RIGGER BALL (CANNONBALL)

Downriggers allow boat anglers to fish deep-running lures with
relatively light tackle.

relatively light tackle and without
heavy sinkers on your main line.

To get a clue as to where to set
your cannonball, you might rely
on a sonar unit, often known as a
graph, depth-finder, or (ugh) fish-
finder. These are valuable tools,
especially in big water. A graph
not only tells you where bottom
is, it can help pinpoint structure,
letting you follow breaklines. On
big, open water, its main value is
to find bottom and baitfish, and to provide hours of entertainment.

In big water, like the Great Lakes, schools of game fish are often on the
prowl for schools of baitfish, which appear on the screen as a cloud, sometimes small, sometimes vast enough to obliterate all other details. Finding
such a cloud can give a clue as to where to set your rigger ball.

Sometimes your unit will also show game fish, which appear on the
screen as an inverted V. We call these "hooks." This is where the entertain-

Game fish appear as arched "hooks"
on many graphs, while a school of
baitfish looks like a dense cloud.

SCHOOL OF BAITFISH   GAME FISH

ment value comes in, as in, "Good hook at
35 feet! . . . Whoa, baby! . . . Huge hook! . . . Come to
Poppa!"

These announcements draw every angler on the
boat, all crowding around a tiny screen to ooh and ahh
and urge those beauties to hit "my" spoon.

▶ **Many graphs, usually the less expensive ones,
show fish as tiny, to large pixilated "fishies," like the ones
your four-year-old drew that you were obliged to display on the fridge. I suppose it works for some people,
but the cry "Big fishy!" just doesn't sound as grown-up as
"Nice hook!"**

A quality graph also indicates the thermocline.

▶ **The thermocline is a band of water that shows the most dramatic change in temperature.**

Let's say the surface temperature is 69°F. At 10 feet it's 66°F, at 15 feet it's 64°F, at 20 feet it's 61°F, at 25 feet it's 56°F, at 30 feet it's 53°F, and at 40 feet it's 50°F. The thermocline is from 20 to 25 feet, the band showing the greatest *change* in temperature.

Thermoclines are important because they sound scientific and identifying one makes you appear knowledgeable. But aside from that, they also indicate the "comfort zone" for many species of fish; too far above is too warm, too far below is too cold.

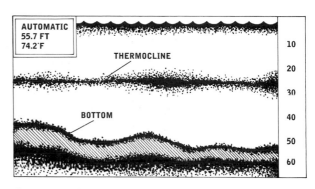

AUTOMATIC
55.7 FT
74.2°F

THERMOCLINE

BOTTOM

10
20
30
40
50
60

On most quality depth-finders, or graphs, the thermocline appears as a band of darker or dust-filled water. The thermocline is often a good place to find fish. Here, it appears between 20 and 30 feet.

▶ **Identifying the thermocline is a good starting point for finding suspended fish in large bodies of water.**

There are a few other gizmos of varying degrees of importance that you may decide to invest in.

Many fish have preferred temperature zones. Chinook salmon, for instance, are happiest in waters around 53°F. And you won't know what the heck the temperature is unless you invest in a temperature probe. Most graphs now monitor the surface temperature, and while a quality graph can indicate where the thermocline is, it doesn't tell you the temperature of it. If you want to know the exact temperature at a specific depth, you've got to spend a few extra bucks.

A "temp" gauge, or probe, is another reel-like gadget you hold in your hand, though some models can be attached to a rigger ball. The weighted probe is lowered to a specific depth and the temperature appears on a readout. In less expensive models, you have to retrieve it quickly and read the temperature on the probe before it warms up. Its value, somewhat like a downrigger, depends on how often you fish big water for suspended fish.

A global positioning system, or GPS, is, among other things, an electronic marker buoy that, unlike the physical buoy, doesn't announce your secret spots to every passing boat.

More important, this gizmo tells you, in exact degrees of latitude and longitude, where you are at any given moment. It can be a lifesaver on big water. As long as you note where you started from, you can find your way home. In emergencies, you can use your radio or cell phone to tell rescuers *exactly* where to find you.

And, you can use your GPS to return the next day to the exact spot

NOT-SO-TALL TALE

Bonanza and Beauty

During the 1970s my passion for steelhead blossomed. (Throughout this book I use rainbows, 'bows, and steelhead interchangeably. In my neck of the woods, all three refer to the anadromous rainbow trout, which spends most of its adult life, except when spawning, in large bodies of water such as the ocean or Great Lakes.) When I was younger, my dad took me out a couple of times in the fall for rainbows. My best one was only 13 inches, which thrilled me at the time, but was dwarfed by the fish we occasionally saw caught by others. For the most part, my family put away their fishing rods at the end of summer.

But in the early to mid-1970s I began hunting 'bows in earnest during the fall. I have had dozens of memorable sessions with them, but two in particular stand out, each for different reasons.

The first was my initial experience with a bonanza in terms of numbers of fish. A friend and I were fishing a popular stretch of river that hosted a good run of 'bows. For some reason, we didn't have any company. It was drizzly and cold, and we were drifting roe bags under old-fashioned (but new at the time) plastic pencil floats. These floats were clunkier than the streamlined versions available today, nearly as bulky as the round "bobbers" they replaced. We didn't even know you had to add enough shot to make them stay vertical; so they drifted along, lying flat.

Suddenly, mine tilted upright and then sank a heartbeat or two later. I set the hook, and a 3-pounder attempted a new high-jump record. My buddy whooped and then joined the fray with a twin to my fish.

In the next few hours we got about a hundred hits between us, landing around forty fish. None of the fish were huge, the largest only about 6 pounds and the average around 2 pounds. But what a lot of fun we had! It was the first time I'd been at the right place at the right time when a fresh school of steelies were moving upstream. It's happened a few times where you hit a school of rampaging salmon. If you luck into a great piece of offshore structure, a GPS makes finding it again a piece of cake.

If you troll a lot, without riggers, you'll occasionally need your hands free for other duties. Rod holders that can be adjusted to various angles and mounted to the side of the boat come in handy. Just be sure your drag is set perfectly. (More on drag settings on pages 131–32.)

There are other gadgets out there, such as dissolved oxygen content meters or pH meters, that appeal mostly to fishin' technicians or to those whose Heightened Awareness has reached near-terminal status.

since, but never with that duration or with that number of fish.

My mind's eye still relishes the pictures of those strange, flat-laying floats, slowly tilting upright before slipping out of sight.

The other memorable rainbow excursion during this time occurred with my brother-in-law Ken. It was around Christmas, and we'd visited a pub and were back at his place drinking coffee. Around midnight, one of us suggested trying some night fishing for 'bows. Neither of us had ever tried it before, but it seemed a fine idea.

A half-hour later we were parked on the dead-end dirt road near our favorite stream at the time. We skirted the edge of a cornfield and entered a narrow band of woods. It was a bright night, quite cold, and we wondered if the creek might be frozen over. It had been nearly a month since we'd fished it. After leaving the woods we had about 200 yards of field to cross before reaching the creek.

I'll never forget leaving the relative dark-ness of the trees to catch my first glimpse of what lay beyond. The full moon broke from behind some thin clouds and reflected off the snow lightly carpeting the field. It was almost blindingly bright. Beyond the field was the creek, a ribbon of diamonds in the dark.

I felt a reverential awe, as if I'd just entered God's own cathedral. We were on a slight rise, and a half-mile to the south we saw Lake Ontario, into which the creek emptied. The moon reflected off the water. Only the sky was relatively dark, those spaces between the twinkling stars.

The creek was unfrozen except near the banks, and we flipped our roe bags into a pool, then set about building a fire. Ken and I fell into a comfortable silence. For an hour or so there was no sign of life in the water. Then a small swirl indicated that at least one finned companion was in the vicinity.

About 3 A.M., Ken's line finally twitched. After a short but spirited tussle, he landed a 14-inch rainbow.

But that night's cake needed no icing. ◄◄

The one that really gets my mono in a backlash, though, is the "color indicator," which purports to determine the best lure color to use on any given day. It's based on water clarity, the species you're after, available light, and what you had for lunch the day before.

Puh-leeze!

After forty years on the water, I think I'm perfectly capable of making the wrong color choice all by myself.

A Confession

It was very difficult to write the sections on what an angler needs. And not just because of my forty years of Awareness-Heightening.

I also suffer from an acute case of Boy Scout Syndrome. I was never a scout, but the motto Be Prepared resonated within me as a universal truth the instant I heard it.

If Armageddon occurs while I'm fishing, I'd still have a decent chance of survival. A tornado could not lift me off my feet when I'm wearing my vest. But even with my vest laden with pounds of miscellaneous gear, I still carry a bulging shoulder bag while fishing streams or rivers.

My bag holds enough worms for four days of fishing. (I never outgrew that What-If-We-Run-Out childhood fear.) It has a spare reel or two, needle-nose pliers (in case I lose my forceps), a priest (more on that later), every jar of salmon eggs and flavored marshmallows I've purchased in the last 15 years, three cases of spinners, plugs, and spoons that are too big for my vest, granola and chocolate bars (some of these go back a few years too), a spare worm blower or two, several packages of hooks and sinkers in case one of my vest pockets comes up empty, a plastic bag or two for roe or a take-home fish, a first-aid kit (accidents happen), sunscreen, insect repellent, and a folding knife.

Every couple years I ruthlessly cull the contents of my vest and bag to discard the junk. Usually, I can lighten each of them by several ounces. Most of this is in the form of granola bar wrappers, discarded lengths of line, and empty hook and sinker packs. I often find, to my great delight, a small bag or two of something I bought at the tackle store and tucked away to sort through later.

I once listened to a talk show that featured a psychiatrist. He said that people who try to prepare for every possible eventuality are neurotic. I had to laugh. Obviously this guy was never a boy scout—or a fisherman.

I am lucky to live on a street that borders a field. A two-minute stroll through that field brings me to a nice creek that boasts a good annual run of rainbows, browns, and salmon. (Actually, it wasn't luck at all. As my wife toured the house with the real-estate agent, I stood rooted in the driveway, staring at the creek, my mind made up. Location, location, location.)

As you might imagine, I fish there quite often. First, I slip on my hip waders, then, over several layers of clothing (the fish run when it's cold), I don my three-quarter-length parka before struggling into my vest (it's handy to have a family member around at this point). My sunglasses, hat, and fingerless gloves complete the ensemble.

Shoulder bag in place, rod and reel in one hand, steel thermos of coffee in the other, I clomp confidently down the street.

All modesty aside, I must cut quite a dashing figure, because no matter how many times the neighbors have seen me over the years, they always stop what they're doing to watch me go by. Kids stare in open-mouthed wonder. The adults smile, wave, and wish me luck, eyes shining with what I can only assume is admiration.

I would wave back, but I am too heavily burdened to lift my arms. So I smile and nod.

Bringing joy to others.

Yet another unexpected bonus to being an angler.

▶ **In retrospect, it seems that only when it comes to fishing am I really prepared. The rest of my life has pretty much caught me off guard.**

The Author strikes a heroic pose before heading out to do battle.

HELEN BARON

CHAPTER 7

Common Sense

Fishing should be a pleasurable activity, not a dangerous one. Yet the mortality statistics for our pastime are frightening. Heightened Awareness shouldn't totally preclude common sense (unless, of course, you're shopping for tackle).

A few simple precautions can help ensure your next outing won't be your last.

For years I resisted wearing a life jacket. I always had one in the boat, because the law demanded it, but except in severe weather I wouldn't wear it. Over time I became a father and insisted that my sons wear them whenever we went out in the boat. Some sample conversations:

"Put on your life jacket."

"OK, but why aren't you wearing yours?"

"I can swim."

"Oh."

A few years later:

"Put on your life jackets."

"But we can swim now."

"Put them on anyhow."

"Why aren't you wearing yours?"

"Uh, I'm more experienced."

"Oh. OK."

The truth was, my life jacket was bulky, uncomfortable, and I couldn't get my fishing vest on over it.

A couple of years ago, we were watching the news. One report was on finding the bodies of two missing fishermen. The announcer solemnly intoned that neither body had on a life jacket.

My youngest son asked me if I thought those dead fishermen were experienced.

I think I muttered, "I don't know."

He said he thought I should wear mine from now on.

In a sudden fit of sanity, I promised him I would.

My life jacket was ten or twelve years old, though, so I went shopping for a new one. What a revelation! Now referred to as PFDs (personal flotation devices), newer models are light, streamlined, and best of all, many have pockets!

I realized that in the boat I mostly used my fishing vest because I kept my line clippers on a chain on the front for easy access. I simply attached another pair to my PFD and hung my fishing vest on the back of my seat so other goodies are still near to hand.

Now I wear it every time I'm in a boat—without exception. I'm no longer a hypocrite, and my sons feel better. If your excuses were similar to mine, please go shopping. At the risk of sounding maudlin, if this book convinces even a handful of anglers to wear a flotation vest *every* time they are in a boat, I'll feel I've accomplished something worthwhile.

Too many male anglers fall overboard while leaning out to answer a call of nature.

If the water is warm, *if* the angler can swim, and *if* another person can operate the boat, he may have an embarrassing, but ultimately amusing, story.

If the water is cold, or the angler is alone, he may become another gruesome statistic. Talk to any conservation officer, marine police officer, or coast guard official and he or she can tell you about recovering bodies in a partial state of undress. It's a very silly and unnecessary reason to die.

Karl and I always carry what we delicately refer to as a "pissoir." Ours is an old, porcelain coffeepot with a convenient handle. No need to lean over

Best Grab by a Non-Shortstop

Dad and I still fished together with some degree of regularity. One day we went to a pond we'd fished occasionally over the years. The outflow from this pond spilled over a narrow 12-foot-high dam and under a two-lane road. After fishing on top for a while, we decided to try the pool under the road.

It was a difficult hole to fish. We could wade only partway in because it got too deep too quickly. It took a longish cast to reach the head of the pool, which was tricky because of the concrete overhead and to the sides. It was like fishing in a large culvert. To further complicate matters, some yahoos had somehow managed to partially submerge a picnic table on the left side, the side I was fishing.

Dad was still rigging up when I made my first cast. *Boom!* In seconds I connected with what turned out to be a lovely 16-inch brown. We had no net, but I managed to back out of the pool and ease it onto the bank.

I'm not sure whether Dad was working out a tangle or what, but I rebaited and cast again while he was still otherwise occupied.

A heavy fish hit immediately. I set the hook and knew I was into a dandy. Whooping and floundering in the thigh-deep water, I desperately tried to keep the fish from going where I *knew* it wanted to go—into that picnic table. I cranked my drag up and prayed my 6-pound test would hold. At least once I felt the fish make contact with the picnic table, and I was

sure that in seconds it would wrap the line around it and the game would be over. My luck held, though, and in a couple of minutes I had worked the fish into the area below the table, closer to me. It surfaced once at this point, without actually jumping, but the size of the boil it made kept my heart in my throat. Now, when it seemed possible that I might actually have a chance to land it, I wondered how on earth we'd manage. I cursed myself for leaving the net in the car. There was no time to fetch it. We usually fished in the pond above, at a place where the bank sloped gently, which made landing a fish simple. I didn't trust my line to hold if it came down to dragging the fish onto the bank, and the fast current made a hand-landing a difficult prospect, as well.

Difficult, but not impossible. I finally eased the fish out of the culvert area, and Dad made a brilliant two-handed grab. A few seconds later, we were grinning at each other, shaking hands, and admiring a beautiful, butter-colored 23-inch native brown. To date, that's still my largest native brown, though I've lost a couple of bruisers in the pond above.

I'd made two casts and caught one nice fish and one terrific one. I quit after that and just watched Dad fish for a while. If I recall correctly, he got a nice 14-incher and, possibly, another smaller one. But what remains in my memory bank is that suddenly sinister picnic table and my dad's desperate and triumphant grab.

the side. It's heavy enough not to blow out of the boat while it's being hauled on the trailer, and it doubles as a bailer.

A pail or a bucket would be more serviceable for women and can be stowed under a seat or weighted with your anchor so it doesn't blow away.

Rifle your cupboards or visit your department store, but investing in a "pissoir" will make a day on the water much more pleasant and much less dangerous.

In chapter 5, I talked about *not* fishing in a thunderstorm. Anglers constantly have to be aware of the weather and have a realistic assessment of the abilities of their boat and its captain. Three-foot swells may mean nothing if you're in a 22-footer. But it means "go home" if you've got a 12-foot aluminum boat. This means using your judgment. It also means that you shouldn't impair that judgment with alcohol.

Bad weather can spring up quickly, and distant but fast-approaching thunder may not be heard over the noise of your engine.

▶ **Get into the habit of regularly scanning the horizon the full 360 degrees.**

If you see ominous clouds, track them. Don't assume that the wind you are experiencing on the water is blowing the clouds in the same direction. Quite often, surface and aerial winds are vastly different.

Listen to the weather forecast for the area you are planning to fish the evening before you leave and again in the morning. (Just don't bet your life that it's accurate.)

If conditions are borderline when you arrive, stay close to the launch site, a marina, or shore so safety isn't far if the weather worsens.

A storm isn't the only weather situation that demands caution. Dense fog can be deadly. If you venture out into a heavy fog you can become disoriented in seconds. Even if you are very experienced in navigating by compass, you'll need radar to pick up floating logs before you smack them.

An experience I had one recent summer was a sobering reminder of how dangerous fog can be.

I was at the family cottage and preparing for my usual predawn outing.

The fog was dense, but, having fished there for thirty years, I knew the lake like the back of my hand and assumed the rising sun would burn it off within a half-hour or so.

I set out very slowly along the shoreline until I judged I was opposite my destination, a shoal in the middle of a mud flat across the lake. The lake is long and narrow, dotted with inlets and bays. Normally the crossing would only take 30 seconds or so, but I was crawling along at trolling speed because of the fog, so I anticipated about a five-minute crossing. Thirty yards out from the shoreline, it became invisible.

I want to reinforce the fact that I had fished this area, which is within a mile of my cottage, hundreds of times. Before this morning, I would have made a sizable wager that I could get there blindfolded.

My crossing went from 5 minutes to 10 and then 20, and the world was a featureless, uniform gray. The sun should have burned off the fog by now, but it seemed that this morning it had decided not to rise at all. I was becoming unsettled, but far from panicking, when finally a dock came into view along with the cottage it belonged to—a totally unfamiliar dock and cottage.

I considered stopping there to wait for the day to lighten. It was much too early to even consider waking the occupants to ask for directions. Besides, by now I was embarrassed enough that I didn't want to turn it into humiliation.

I decided to follow the shoreline slowly until some feature became recognizable so that I could reorient myself. By the time I came to a floating dock I recognized, I had been on the water for nearly an hour. I was about 2 miles in the *opposite* direction from where I was headed *and* on the *other* side of the lake from where I thought I was.

Another twenty minutes of puttering along the shoreline brought me back to my starting point, my own dock.

A wiser person than I would have stopped at this point, gone inside for some breakfast, and waited for the fog to lift.

I have rarely been accused of being wise.

The water was as calm as glass, the light penetration, obviously, was nil. I just *knew* that the walleye were enjoying an extended feed at that shoal, if I could just get there.

Heartened by the sight of familiar surroundings, I set off once again, absolutely certain that *this* time I would have no problem. I decided that I hadn't hugged my side of the shoreline long enough before setting off across the lake. So I went on for an extra minute or so before making my five-minute crossing.

Fifteen minutes later, the shoreline gradually revealed itself, along with a dying birch tree I recognized. I was on the correct side of the lake and only about 1 mile west of my target. I turned and crawled along the shore until my shoal crept into sight.

I got skunked, of course. Conditions remained "perfect" for another two hours, but I went fishless, and, in retrospect, deservedly so. The fog lifted at about 11 a.m., and I went back to the cottage. I regaled my family with my tale, which *was* somewhat amusing in hindsight.

But the truth of the matter is that what I did was dumb. If I had been any less familiar with the lake, I may have allowed my unease to develop into panic. I may have opened up the throttle to get somewhere, anywhere, faster. I could very well have hit a floating log or unmarked shoal.

It seems obvious, but I think worth stating, that you should familiarize yourself with, and obey, your state or provincial marine laws. They vary to some extent, but most have these rules in common: have an approved life jacket or flotation device for everyone on board, and a bailing can and a pair of oars or paddles, as well as a whistle, air horn, flare, or other emergency signaling device. Depending on the size of your craft, you may also be required to have a fire extinguisher, running lights, and a radio.

If you wear your life jacket, are sensible about weather conditions, and don't pee over the side of the boat, chances are your tombstone won't read "Died Doing What He Loved."

CHAPTER **8**

Etiquette and Ethics

Etiquette

We've all seen the unruly child in the restaurant or supermarket who wreaks havoc while the parents look on in benign ignorance. They think the word "no" may damage their dear little darling's delicate sensibilities.

You can't blame the child. He doesn't know any better. He has not been properly trained.

Interest in our pastime is booming. A lot of anglers are coming into the world of fishing as adults, never having fished with Dad or Grandpa.

They've seen the TV programs. They've read the magazines. They have the waders, the vest, the rods and reels. They may even know how to use them properly. They look and talk and smell like *real* anglers.

▶ **But some anglers consistently break the cardinal rule of fishing courtesy: respecting another angler's space.**

It mostly happens on streams and rivers.

You've assessed a nice little pool, determined the current speed and the area where your quarry is likely to be hiding. You approached it carefully, keeping your shadow behind you, walking softly, and you have found the perfect little garden worm to fool the trout. You've made a couple of false casts, gauging the distance and wind effect, when one of two things happens.

A bull moose in waders and vest crashes across the stream, 3 feet above *your* hole, sending a cascade of mud, pebbles, and roily water to spook *your* fish.

Or some yahoo arrives and repeatedly fires a huge, rattling plug through the pool, spoiling any possibility of your making a successful drift.

This problem usually manifests itself on popular fisheries. One such example would be the predictable runs of migratory fish on easily accessible rivers. Word spreads like wildfire, and soon it seems that the anglers out-number the fish three to one.

Some larger pools can host several anglers *if* they're using the same techniques in a predictable pattern. If four anglers are drifting roe bags under pencil floats, please don't be the fifth guy who shows up and lobs spinners. You will not be popular.

Many smaller holes and riffles can only be comfortably fished by one angler. Even if you can *see* the 10-pound rainbow he's trying to catch, even if you've *never, ever* caught a 10-pound rainbow and would *really, really* like to—*leave him alone!* Find another hole. Go away. That guy who doesn't want your company is me.

Very popular stretches of water often have dozens of anglers fishing shoulder-to-shoulder. I usually avoid these scenes, but if you want to join the party, first wait for a reasonable opening and watch what the anglers are doing. Prepare to do the same. Note their rhythm and fall into it. Always respect the cry of "Fish on!" and reel in immediately.

Even seasoned anglers occasionally experience tangled lines in these situations. If it's your fault, apologize. If it's not, forgive. And don't leave your sense of humor at home.

There are rules of etiquette on open water too, and these also usually involve space. If someone is anchored and working over a shoal, DON'T troll within 10 feet and then offer a cheerful wave. The angler may respond with only part of a hand.

Say somebody fishing 200 yards away lands a nice walleye and tosses a marker buoy into the water. This is not an invitation to "come on over." It's the angling equivalent of a dog lifting a hind leg and marking a tree. It's about establishing territory. Respect it or prepare to fight—on second thought, just respect it.

If you're having a terrible day and that guy's marker buoy is acting like a beacon, there's no reason you can't hover within a respectful distance, say a hundred yards or so.

But if the other angler looks your way, try to cast while cringing and wag your stern frantically, like a nice, submissive puppy.

Many times, on larger bodies of water, a popular area attracts a host of boats, called a "pack."

Joining a pack can be a good starting point if you're fishing unfamiliar water. But your approach is still important. Don't roar full speed into the middle of the pack.

▶ **Always respect the space of any angler who's already fishing an area when you arrive.**

Approach the fringe at low speed. Assess what the bulk of the anglers are doing. If they're anchored, they won't appreciate you trolling among them. If they're trolling, they won't want you anchoring in their path.

Do what they are doing, or stay well outside the pack.

Sometimes, fishing on the fringe is more productive anyway because the activity at the center spooks the fish and moves them out of the zone.

We have enough enemies on the water among the Others—power-boaters, skiers, sailors, and those annoying, buzzing snowmobiles that float. We don't need to make more enemies among ourselves.

Another rule of etiquette broken with annoying regularity is not leaving the shores or banks of fisheries as clean or cleaner than when we arrive.

Don't discard garbage. And *never* throw away discarded line. It takes forever to degrade, can fatally entangle wildlife, and fouls the bottom. It's a simple matter to take along a plastic bag in which to stow your own garbage as well as that left behind by others less considerate. Many private landowners deny access to all anglers because a few slobs left their litter behind.

Ethics
Killing Fish

How do you want to die?

Few of us would choose slow suffocation, sometimes after hours of suffering. I'll bet not a single hand would rise in favor of being disemboweled while fully conscious.

But that's how too many so-called anglers kill their fish.

One of my favorite sayings about our sport is that the amount of time we spend fishing is not deducted from our life spans. I would love for this to be true, as I have a few years in the bank. But no matter how much time we spend on the water, sooner or later the guy with the scythe is going to knock on our door. And we'll be home.

When contemplating the manner of our own death, most of us think of two words: "quick" and "painless." If a friend or loved one is terminally ill, we may pray that God takes them this way.

We exercise godlike power over every fish we catch. We can release them or we can keep them.

▶ **If we choose to keep fish, we also must choose the manner of their death. Make it quick and painless.**

The older I get, the more shades of gray I see in my moral spectrum. But some things *are* black and white.

Tossing a fish up on the bank to suffocate is wrong.

Killing coarse fish like chub or suckers, just because they aren't the trout we are hoping for, is wrong.

Towing fish around on a stringer is wrong.

If, at the end of the day, they are then allowed to suffocate at the bottom of the boat, it's *doubly* wrong.

Confining a fish in a dark, tiny, noisy live well for hours, only to kill it afterward is wrong.

If you are going to keep fish for the table, quickly dispatch them with a billy club or "priest" (to administer last rites). Then, if you're fishing from a boat or within an easy walk of your car, put your fish in a plastic bag on ice in a cooler.

NOT-SO-TALL TALE

Night Eyes

Late one October in the mid 1970s, word filtered through the angling grapevine that nice catches of walleye were being made below a dam about 50 miles north of my home. Brother-in-law Ken and I decided to investigate. The dam and river were in the middle of a public park in a small town. We arrived at about four in the afternoon. There was a sizable crowd of wader-clad anglers fishing directly below the dam and quite a few others along the bank behind them. The crowd thinned about a hundred yards below the dam where the deeper water turned to shallower rapids.

Those working the deeper water nearest the dam seemed to be evenly split between anglers drifting minnows along bottom, or under a float, and those firing plugs and retrieving with the current.

I had waders but no minnows, and even at that relatively young age I didn't relish fishing in a crowd, so I decided to work the shallower rapids below.

It was my first experience fishing for fast-water walleye, and I was at a bit of a loss. I had a few jigs with me, including some of those newfangled Mr. Twisters with the plastic curly-tailed grub bodies. I tied one on and cast the jig diagonally upstream, bouncing it back and across to me. Over the next few hours and into the evening I caught several small walleye, none larger than 16 inches. But I was happy with the lures and knew I'd found a permanent addition to my arsenal. I also left more than a few jigs as souvenirs on the rocky bottom.

By 11 P.M. I was getting tired and resting on the bank as often as I was casting. It was a pleasant night, with the temperature in the low 50s (Fahrenheit). Ken wandered back and forth from the dam to where I was. He'd gotten a few fish too, but nothing to write home about.

I switched to a 5-inch floating Rapala around midnight. I wanted it to run a little deeper than it normally would, so I added a medium-sized split shot. But I began my retrieves as soon as it hit water because those

▶ **Killing your fish quickly and putting it on ice is not only humane, it prevents the flesh from deteriorating. You'll be able to taste the results.**

A good priest is usually made of hardwood and should be of sufficient size and heft to subdue your target fish. A sawn-off broom handle will work for smallish trout or walleye, but it's inadequate for larger fish. Small souvenir baseball bats are good, though, as are axe handles or chair legs (if they are rounded).

Unless the fish is too large to hold, don't lay it on the bank or the bottom of the boat when you hit it, as this will dissipate the force of the blow, re-

lure-eating rocks were only about 3 feet down.

At a little after 1 A.M. I found one of those rocks. Or so I thought until it began to move. I was finally into a heavy fish, which, combined with the strong current, shifted my imagination into overdrive in no time. After several minutes of stubborn refusal to "come to Papa," I began to win the battle. Soon after, Ken helped me land my biggest walleye up to that time. It measured 29 inches and probably weighed 8 pounds or so.

There's a postscript. Around 3 A.M. we decided to try another fast-water area about 40 miles away from this one. This place was even more crowded, and the area we decided to fish required a long cast from where we stood.

I lost my last couple jigs in short order. And I couldn't get the Rapalas out far enough, so by the time the sun rose I had rigged a pretty outlandish concoction of a slip-sinkered 6-inch purple plastic worm rigged with two hooks.

Much to my amazement, on my third cast something clobbered it. Even though the current was heavier than where I'd caught my other walleye, I knew this was also a very big fish. Could lightning strike twice? Could I catch the biggest walleye of my life, only to have it dwarfed by an even larger one hours later?

Nearly a half-hour passed before the fish was close enough to see, and by this time the battle had attracted quite a crowd.

I didn't know whether to laugh or cry when the carp became visible. It wasn't long before we were all laughing, though. He was a good fish, about 15 or 16 pounds, and had the hook fairly in his mouth. I've since caught carp that hit lures, but until that time had considered them to be only catchable on bottom-fished, motionless bait. So it never once entered my mind while fighting that fish that I was dealing with a carp. In my mind, it was either a record-breaking walleye or a very nice muskie. Oh, well.

Another deposit in the knowledge bank. Another addition to the story list. Another unforgettable fishing adventure. ◄█

quiring you to administer several additional shots. If you're right-handed, hold the fish in your left hand, with your thumb depressing its dorsal fin and your fingers around its belly (reverse if left-handed). Hold the fish firmly, as they're slippery critters.

Strike it with at least two sharp blows to the top of the skull. The first one should stun or kill it. The second is insurance. With experience, you can unhook, kill, and put a fish on ice in less than 30 seconds.

If you're fishing moving water from land and covering a lot of ground, then obviously lugging around a cooler is a teensy bit impractical. There are a couple of ways to keep fish fresh under these circumstances.

If you're after small trout or other small fish, they can be kept in a creel. Usually made of wicker, willow, or split bamboo, creels are worn over the shoulder and allow air to flow through and around the fish. On warm days, dampen some ferns to put around your catch. Evaporation has a cooling effect. If it's going to be a long, hot day, gut the fish after you kill it. This will greatly retard spoilage.

If you're after bigger game and the air temperature is above 50°F, take along a *doubled* plastic bag big enough for your catch. Kill your fish, bag it, and place it in shallow water while you fish. The water will keep it cool, and the doubling is to ensure that no water leaks in, which would soften and spoil the flesh. If the air temperature is below 50°F, just bag the fish after killing it, and put it in the shade on shore.

If you're going to spend a full day fishing, convince yourself before you start that anything you catch in the first half of the day gets released. You don't want to lug around a heavy bag all day, and a fresher fish is a tastier fish. If you must keep a fish for several hours, remember to gut it after you kill it, then bag it.

How to Gut a Fish

Gutting a fish is a simple procedure, but a sharp knife helps. Just make a cut up the belly from the anus to the gills and remove the entrails. Scrape and/or rinse any clotted blood. Some anglers also remove the gills. Discard the entrails off the beaten path. Crows, gulls, turtles, and other carrion eaters will make short work of them.

Sometimes people kill fish for reasons other than food; perhaps as fertilizer for the garden or for bait. If they use panfish or coarse fish, and the catch is killed humanely, I can't get too worked up over it. I sometimes kill a small perch for bait.

But a practice that makes me see red is killing salmon and/or trout solely for their roe—which is used for bait—and leaving the carcasses to rot on the bank or in the water.

I mentioned earlier that my "home" creek hosts annual spawning runs of brown trout, steelhead, and chinook salmon. The salmon run, in particular, draws hordes of anglers from all over.

Most of them fish fairly for these giants. Many of them, including me, like to get fresh roe every year for bait. When we catch a female, we stroke its belly firmly, from throat to anus, to see if the eggs are loose. If not, we revive and release the fish. If she has ripe, loose roe, we gather a *portion* in a plastic bag (*never* all of it), then revive and release her.

Some people make a fair amount of money selling roe illegally. These and other so-called "anglers" (I have other, more colorful words for them) want *all* the roe, loose or still in the skein. (Immature roe is tightly encased in a clear membrane called a *skein*.)

The easiest way to get it is to snag the fish illegally, with heavy tackle and gang hooks, land it, gut it, and remove the roe. So that is just what they do. Every fall, I am sickened at the sight of dozens of these once-proud fighters, reduced to gutted, rotting hulks along the banks and in the shallows.

I think the punishment should fit the crime, but most of these miscreants work at night and in gangs, making them difficult and dangerous to apprehend.

▶ **The best deterrent to unethical fishing behavior is education. Set a good example for young and/or neophyte anglers by always treating your catch with respect.**

A common question I get from some Others when I decry this snagging and gutting practice is: "Well, aren't those salmon going to die in a few days or weeks anyway?"

The short answer is yes, they are. Trout can spawn several times, but Pacific salmon such as chinooks and cohos come upstream to spawn and die. By the time these fish have been in a creek or river for a few days, their condition begins to deteriorate. Soon, they become virtually inedible, so killing them to feed you or your family makes no sense.

Their entire lives are spent toward one purpose: to reproduce. To accomplish this, most of them undertake a long, arduous journey from big water to the streams they were born in. They often battle seemingly insurmountable odds with a single-minded determination that is nothing short of heroic.

They are proud, valiant, courageous warriors, and they *deserve* the death they were born to, having accomplished their mission by perpetuating the species.

To interrupt them, as I do, once a year, is enough to cause me some guilt. I ameliorate it by ensuring the female still has most of her eggs and is well enough to continue when released.

To halt their journey, without even the excuse of using them for food, is just plain wrong. To deliberately foul-hook them in order to kill them compounds the crime immeasurably. To gut them alive is unforgivable.

Fishing for Spawners

I mentioned earlier that I don't like to pursue fish I can see. This doesn't extend to pools where a rise or a flash lets me know someone is home. It *does* extend to spawning salmon or trout that are on their "redds" (spawning beds). Redds are usually in shallow water, and the mating couple (and often their attendants) are highly visible.

They aren't interested in eating, but they can be provoked into striking. But please try to resist the urge. Just watching them is a treat.

The ethics of angling for any spawning fish may be debatable, but trying to catch a fish that's guarding its eggs is not. Most species of freshwater fish have no parental responsibility. They court, mate, and either die or go about their business.

But male bass and other members of the sunfish family aggressively guard their eggs and hatchlings for a time.

Closed seasons usually protect these fish, but late spawning can occur, or angling for another species may result in an arm-jarring strike from a protective dad.

If this happens, please go somewhere else to fish. These fish will strike at anything in the area and will do so repeatedly until exhausted. While they're fighting you, and afterward, when they're too spent to defend anything, their eggs are vulnerable to predators. A few minutes of "fun" could mean many fewer bass or sunfish in years to come.

There is no challenge for anglers in exploiting this defensive instinct, and in the long run you'll be cutting your own throat if you do.

Catch and Release

If I caught and released a nice rainbow 25 years ago, eyebrows would rise among many of my fellow anglers. Some would even get angry and demand I give the fish to them if I didn't want it. (If they asked nicely, I sometimes did.)

Fishing used to be solely about catching and keeping.

Gradually, the concept of releasing some, most, or even all of one's catch caught on with most anglers. Any resource will dwindle if not managed properly.

While fish and game departments establish regulations for the fisheries they oversee, releasing a fish to spawn and/or be caught again another day, puts some control of *our* resource where it belongs, in our own hands.

▶ **Practicing some form of catch and release is a practical and logical way to ensure a future fishery for ourselves, our children, and our grandchildren.**

I keep 10 to 15 percent of the fish I catch, mostly walleye and a few trout or small, immature salmon. Few of us depend solely on what we catch or hunt for sustenance, so I can't see the point in keeping every edible fish caught, even if it's within the legal limit for that species.

However, I also have a problem with the angler who *never* keeps a fish. I think it is important to teach our children that not all food mysteriously appears in our refrigerator wrapped in plastic and reclining on a Styrofoam tray.

They need to learn that *something* has to die so we can eat, whether plant or animal. Abstract concepts like "death" and "the food chain" become concrete when you and your children are cleaning your catch. Some of the best discussions I've had with my sons occurred around the cleaning table.

Obviously, it's just as important to teach our children to respect and nourish life when we *aren't* going to eat our catch. This means teaching them the proper way to handle fish in order to increase the odds of survival when released.

▶ **Fish that are played quickly, hooked in the jaw, and unhooked while still in the water have the best chance of survival.**

The tackle you use should be appropriate for the species you are pursuing so you can avoid exhausting fish you plan to release. If the fight is an extended one, you must take the time to revive the fish before release. Hold

Although fun will always be the primary reason for taking kids fishing, the sport is also a springboard for discussions about life, death, and ecology. Left to right: My niece Jenna proudly displays a nice largemouth; my son Jacob with a very respectable smallmouth; and my son Francis with lunch du jour (walleye).

KARL BARON (RIGHT)

the fish upright, facing the current if possible, one hand around the tail and one under the pectoral fins near the upper chest. Now wait. This can be tough to do when the water temperature is only slightly above freezing. But it's necessary. Usually within seconds or minutes, the fish is strong enough to escape your loose grasp.

Next to the sight of my children being born, my biggest thrill is watching a big, beautiful fish swim away.

Surprisingly, some of our biggest and meanest freshwater fish are the most vulnerable to fighting and handling mortality. The fierce demeanor of muskie and pike belie their delicate constitutions.

Use heavy tackle when fishing exclusively for these species, and keep pliers handy so they can be released at the side of the boat. Pinching the barbs on any lure or hook is a good idea if your intention is to release every fish caught. Many muskie anglers use a "cradle," a sort of blanket between two poles, to immobilize big fish while still in the water before trying to unhook them.

If the fish is too exhausted to swim away, support it as described above and move it gently from side to side until it's strong enough to wriggle free.

Netting any very large game fish reduces its chances for survival. A fish that is thrashing around in a net can

DANNY BIRD/ATLANTIC SALMON FEDERATION

Taking the time to revive a fish after a prolonged fight can greatly increase its odds of survival. When sufficiently recovered, the fish will wriggle away from your loose grasp.

To Wet or Not to Wet?

Some anglers believe they need to wet their hands before handling fish, as a dry hand can remove a bit of protective slime from the fish.

Other anglers—including me—as well as some scientists believe that if you wet your hands, you're more likely to squeeze the fish harder in order to keep control of it, possibly causing damage to the fish's internal organs. This is probably especially true of small fish. Most large fish can and should be unhooked while still wholly or partly in the water, which makes this point moot, as your hands are in the water, too.

I never counsel readers to wet their hands first, on the premise that hand-wetting is more likely to hurt the fish than a modest—and temporary—removal of some of their protective slime.

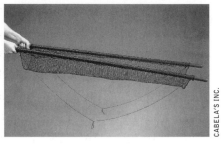

Using a cradle to immobilize and unhook a large fish while still in the water improves its chance of survival considerably. You'll need an extra pair of hands in the boat, though, so make sure you have a buddy along if you're going after big muskie or pike.

tangle lines and hooks, making a longer job of unhooking and releasing. It also removes protective slime, and the thrashing can cause damage to internal organs. Rubberized nets with shallow bags are better than nylon meshed ones if you must net fish that will be released.

When bait fishing, an unwanted fish sometimes swallows the whole offering. Check to ensure that none of the bait is lodged in the fish's throat. If it is, remove the bait with forceps or needle-nose pliers. Then cut your line close to the fish's mouth and release it.

Don't try to remove the hook. If you do, the fish's death is certain. Saving a few pennies to avoid tying on a new hook isn't worth killing any fish.

I have recaught fish released this way, with a bit of line still visible, so they were healthy enough to continue feeding. In time, the fish's stomach acid dissolves the hook.

You can minimize the possibility of gut-hooking a fish by setting the hook early in the bite. If it gets gut-hooked anyway, you can maximize the fish's chance of survival by using small bronzed (not plated) hooks. Many plated hooks (gold, nickel, etc.) are designed to catch the angler's eye and wallet. They don't dissolve as quickly as bronzed steel hooks.

Sometimes you'll hook a fish in the gills or in the back of the tongue and it will be bleeding. A bleeding fish is most likely mortally injured and should be kept for the table. It's cruel to release a fish that is almost certainly facing a slow death. If I mortally injure a tiny or inedible fish, I will remove the hook, kill the fish quickly, and throw it back. Gulls, turtles, or other scavengers will see that it's not wasted.

Sometimes, when pier fishing, for instance, it's impractical to revive a fish by holding it in the water. You're too high above it. In these instances, toss the fish back *headfirst*. The sudden rush of oxygen is revitalizing, and the momentum propels the fish toward bottom and safety.

▶ **Hook removal can be perilous for the unwary angler, too. Always have a pair of needle-nose pliers handy. If you want a recipe for disaster, simply combine one 10-pound pike, two sets of treble hooks, and one bare hand. Add a good thrashing from the pike, and go directly to the nearest emergency room (which is usually a painfully long distance away).**

Tournaments

Although I've toyed with the idea a few times, I have never fished in a tournament, and my feelings about them are mixed.

I wrote earlier that I think it's cruel to keep a fish in a live well for hours, only to kill it later. But keeping a fish in a live well for hours and releasing it later, as they do in tournaments, I file under the heading of "necessary evil." Most tournaments, particularly the large, professional ones we've all seen on television, are well managed and place a premium on releasing healthy fish. Many go so far as to place the fish in large, chemically treated recovery tanks to be released later as close as possible to where they were caught. Virtually all tournaments deduct "ounces" from an angler who weighs in a dead or unreleasable fish.

But no sensible person needs to read studies to deduce that the mortality rate for tournament-released fish exceeds that of fish immediately released boatside.

Overall, however, I believe tournaments do more good than harm to our sport. They promote interest in it and provide a positive economic benefit for many small, rural areas. Profits are often ploughed back into local fisheries programs.

For me, fishing is a quiet, contemplative pastime and not a competitive one. But tournaments have enabled a lot of anglers to make a living doing what they love, and it's hard to argue with that.

I suppose that in my ideal world all tournaments would be judged by total length rather than total weight. Independent spotters aboard each boat would measure and record the length of each fish, which could then be released immediately. But the weigh-ins at these events have become huge crowd-pleasers, so I'm not going to hold my breath.

The Antis

Organizations like PETA (People for the Ethical Treatment of Animals) and other animal welfare groups have recently added sportfishing to the list of activities they're not at all happy with. They are particularly incensed by the concept of catch and release, claiming it is a recurring form of torture for the fish. They cite studies indicating that fish feel pain and claim that the practice of hooking, fighting, and then releasing them, weakened and traumatized, reveals anglers as either unconscionable sadists or ignorant Neanderthals.

I'm neither a sadist nor a scientist. The profundity of my thoughts pose no threat to Stephen Hawking or Jean-Paul Sartre. But I've been fishing for most of my 51 years, my IQ is above room temperature, and I'm observant.

I cannot, with absolute certainty, say that fish feel no pain. But I have seen them batter rocks with their heads and bodies. I've watched them scrape their fins and bellies raw while carving out a redd. I have watched them leap headfirst into concrete walls, lay stunned for a moment, and then do it again.

Many times I have set the hook in the jaws of a large fish that did not react at all for up to a minute; simply holding its position until some nagging, pulling sensation gradually worked its way to the forefront of its consciousness.

Most fish have hard, bony, or cartilaginous jaws—like trout, salmon, muskie, pike, walleye, and bass—or thick, rubbery lips—like suckers or carp. I believe this tissue is analogous to calluses on our hands or feet, not completely impervious to pain, but relatively insensitive. As an example, more than once I've been trolling with a plug with up to four sets of treble hooks. Any bait fisherman is familiar with the tap-tap or chomp-chomp feeling that indicates a fish is biting. I've experienced that same sensation from pike *chewing* on my plug!

▶ **I firmly believe that a fish fights when hooked, not because it is in agony, but because it is being tugged in a direction it has no intention of going.**

Being hooked results in frantic swimming that seems to be an instinctual flight response; I believe the hook causes a discomfort similar to a bit in a horse's mouth.

"OK," Others out there might be saying, "let's, just for the moment, concede the point of physical pain. However, you *do* admit to panic, which is traumatic, a kind of psychic pain."

Yes, I believe most fish panic when hooked. But to believe that panic inevitably leads to trauma is, I think, inaccurate.

Fish don't dwell on the past. Unlike humans, they are incapable of playing the "coulda, shoulda, woulda" game. They have no concept of time. Let me just slide into a fish's head for a moment and relate what I believe a hooked fish's thought processes might be:

"Food! . . . Eat . . . Danger! . . . Flight! . . . Fear! . . . Gone . . . Rest."

I cannot count the number of times I have hooked the same fish twice, often within minutes. If they were traumatized, it sure was short-term.

And then there's the tale of The Rock Bass.

Many years ago, I anchored over a ledge on our cottage lake. I was still-fishing with worms, primarily for walleye or smallmouth bass. I was casting into about 20 feet and bringing the bait slowly back to boatside, which was sitting over about 9 or 10 feet of water.

Directly under the boat I got a bite, set the hook, and reeled in a spunky rock bass. It was bigger than average, well over a pound, and had a distinctive, fully healed old scar near its tail, probably a souvenir of nearly being a meal for a pike or walleye. I released it and continued fishing.

Within a few minutes I had another bite and reeled in the same fish. After a chuckle, I gave it a mild scolding and then released it again.

Ten minutes later, this supremely untraumatized fish bit yet again. This time, I think it swam *toward* the boat, so we could speed up the unhooking and releasing part of the game. After this third time, I raised anchor and left.

For years, The Rock Bass was just an amusing story. But in light of the attacks over catch-and-release angling, it has become an important one. This was *not* some weak fish, desperate for a morsel to stay alive. It was in prime condition, sleek, fat, and healthy. It was *not* aggressively defending a spawning site. I caught it in August (well past May spawning time here) and in relatively deep water.

Was it an extremely stupid fish? Perhaps. But not stupid enough to die young in a hostile environment that preys on any weakness. The rock bass was several years old.

What I took from this incident was the knowledge that a final word can be added to the list of fish thoughts I fantasized about above: "Forget."

Fish that are released in good condition often forget their "ordeal" and go on about their business.

Which is good news for them and good news for anglers.

I think the work of animal welfare groups in opening the public's eyes to the horrible cruelties perpetrated on animals in cosmetic and product testing is admirable. It is laudable that they have raised awareness of the living and testing conditions of laboratory animals everywhere. I appreciate their attempts to protect endangered species, although I disagree with some of their methods.

If they were to target and expose the small percentage of "slob" fishermen and hunters, I would support them wholeheartedly.

But they are misguided and, I believe, misinformed when they set their

JUSTIN HOFFMAN

Quick, proper releases ensure that beauties like this smallmouth can live to breed—and fight—another day.

sights on a large group of conservation-minded men and women enjoying age-old outdoor activities.

Some of the more radical elements within these groups would ban any sort of fishing, including catch and keep.

I will apologize for killing and eating a portion of my catch when vegetarians apologize for hacking the heads off cauliflowers, yanking carrots from their homes, and ripping apples off trees. All are living things, all are killed so people can eat.

CHAPTER **9**

Favorite Fish and Special Tactics

Favorite Fish

When it comes to my favorite fish, I subscribe to the theory, "if you can't be with the one you love, love the one you're with."

Most of my fishing outings are aimed at catching either walleye or steelhead (rainbows). But while walleye fishing, I often make incidental contact with muskie, pike, or small and largemouth bass, depending on the water I am fishing that day.

And while steelhead fishing, I often lock horns with brown trout and salmon, even the occasional lake trout. I don't find this upsetting. For me, it's a little like showing up for a blind date and finding four beautiful women waiting instead of just one.

I love walleye because they're mysterious and moody and unexcelled in the frying pan. Plodding, sluggish fighters, much like lake trout, they still give a decent account of themselves on light tackle. To the unappreciative eye they will win no beauty contests with those milky, protruding eyes and rather drab coloration. But they have "wonderful personality" and are always welcome at the end of my line.

They are an adaptable fish, as my two favorite walleye fishing spots demonstrate. The first spot is the lake I've mentioned throughout this book, the one where my family has a cottage. It's a deep, clear, Canadian Shield lake, and most of the walleye are caught on bottom-bouncing, live-bait rigs or jigs, in 15 to 25 feet of water.

The second fishing spot, also mentioned earlier, is near my home. It is a shallow lake, weed-choked and with an average depth of about 8 feet. Many of the walleye we catch there come from only about 4 feet of water. The habitat and, consequently, the techniques used are vastly different from the first lake. But the fish, bless their cold little hearts, are the same.

At our cottage lake, smallmouth bass inhabit many of the same feeding zones as walleye, and they are not at all reluctant to smack our offerings. To me, only the steelhead rivals a smallie when it comes to combining spectacular leaps with bulldog determination. Smallies in the 2-pound range are particularly crazed, often breaking the surface five or six times before tuckering themselves out. The bigger ones, the 3-plus-pounders, will usually only waste energy on one jump, and if that fails to dislodge the hook, they will slug it out toe-to-toe, never conceding an inch. Their eagerness to hit and their never-say-die fighting abilities make them special.

Every once in a while a pike takes a liking to what's on the menu. Most are in the 2- to 6-pound range in the cottage lake and my largest ran about 12 pounds. (Both Karl and I have tangled with a *much* bigger one. That story comes a little later on.) The only time I'm disappointed with finding a pike on the end of my line is when I've been fooled into thinking I have a great walleye. They fight very hard

On good days, double-headers (two anglers connecting with fish at the same time) are common. Here, I'm holding the results of one such event—a pair of nice walleye.

A decent smallmouth is always a treat.

KARL BARON

My brother Mark triumphantly shows off his "trophy" pike.

in the initial stages of combat, often belying their size. Halfway to the boat, they seemingly surrender, approaching rather meekly. Don't be fooled. Just as you reach out with hand or net they'll erupt, spraying you with water and testing your drag.

On the other, shallower lake we fish, muskie and largemouth bass are often incidental catches. Anyone who has experienced the savage strike, furious battle, and toothy glare of a muskie quickly joins the fan club. Although I have never specifically targeted them, the two or three we latch onto nearly every time out are always thrilling, and I half expect one with every cast. The muskies in this lake average about 6 to 10 pounds, and my largest was about 20 pounds. Our encounters with these fish have caused me to beef up my tackle to reduce the stress of a prolonged fight. The water in this lake is usually stained (discolored), so the heavier line doesn't diminish my success with walleye.

Appearances aside, muskies are a relatively slow-growing, delicate fish that aren't great in the frying pan. I release all I catch, as does every other angler I know. They're too special a fish to keep, unless of course you've latched on to that new world-record 70-plus-pounder.

JUSTIN HOFFMAN

The muskie's fierce demeanor hides a rather delicate constitution. Use heavy tackle to shorten the fight with these great fish.

That same shallow, weedy lake is a largemouth angler's dream, yet the species is severely *under*fished. Our American cousins would shake their heads and call it a travesty. But in Canada, the walleye is king, the muskie a distant second, and the largemouth barely shows up on the radar. There are hundreds of acres of lily pads, reeds, and slop that rarely see an angler's line.

Although Karl and I usually fish areas that are less-than-classic largemouth water (i.e., the deeper, outside weed beds and edges), we pick up the occasional decent largemouth of up to 5 pounds. No doubt, there are much larger ones around. I wish I could say that catching a good large-mouth makes their appeal to my southern friends crystal clear, but I can't. After a short slugfest they seem almost eager to come to the boat so they can be released. I *do* very much enjoy their pugnacious hits, though, and will never turn one down.

Migratory rainbow trout, or steel-head, have a very special place in my heart. The blonde bombshell of the fishing world, the rainbow is dazzling, wild, beautiful, and unpredictable. When caught in big water, where they spend most of their adult lives, they are gleaming silver slabs of mus-cle. If caught in the lower rivers, especially pre-spawn, their many dots and character-istic crimson slash appear, adding immea-surably to their beauty.

Steelhead are strong, acrobatic fighters, capable of long, line-stripping runs. The middling-sized fish, the 2- to 8-pounders, are particularly spectacular. They don't just jump. They hurtle across the top of the water for yards, making your drag scream for mercy, then turn on a dime and charge toward you before

JUST'N HOFFMAN

A chunky largemouth taken from the type of cover bass love.

Karl shows off a handsome steelhead caught in early fall.

shattering the surface with a cartwheeling leap, followed in quick succession by a triple Lutz and a resounding belly flop. All you can do in these instances is madly retrieve your slack line and hope the fish is still there when it tightens. Often, it is not, and you rebait with fingers that seem like they'll never stop shaking. There's not much you can do after one of these incredible displays of hook throwing except shake your head, smile, and applaud the victor.

Chinook and coho salmon, as well as brown trout, are often incidental catches while fishing for 'bows in my home waters.

Coho average in the "teens" in weight and are every bit as spectacular as rainbows. They are usually caught while casting or trolling spoons or plugs, and they're a special treat because they are relatively rare.

Their bigger, brawnier cousin, the chinook, is much more plentiful. Adult chinook average in the mid-20s, and 30-plus-pounders are common. While not ordinarily jumpers, chinook are powerful, line-stripping fighters. It is not uncommon to hear an angler say he was "spooled" by a chinook—the fish stripped every inch of 400-odd yards of 20-pound line. When caught from a boat, the angler must be prepared to chase the fish. If caught from a pier, the angler can only run to the end and pray. No one who wrestles with a chinook will forget the feeling of their throbbing arms and thumping heart. Like the coho, chinook are often taken on spoons and plugs. Pier or break-wall anglers also get their share on roe, worms, or marshmallows.

If you catch three or four hefty chinook (like this one) in a day, your arms won't be much good for anything else for a while.

The big-water browns can be as cautious and tough to fool as their smaller, stream-dwelling brothers. They average 6 to 10 pounds in these parts, but 20-pounders are taken every year. Most are caught by casting or trolling spoons or plugs on light line. Many are taken every fall in the mouths or harbors of tributaries when preparing to spawn.

When actually in the streams or rivers, all the trout and salmon are susceptible to roe, worms, flies, spinners, and plugs.

For the multispecies angler, which includes most of us, it's as hard to pick a favorite fish as it is to pick a favorite child. Every time my rod bends and I feel life on the other end, my face freezes in a huge grin no matter what the species.

Karl with a chunky pre-spawn brown.

Special Tactics
Slack Lines = More Fish

"Tight lines!"

Those words have become a fishing catch phrase, synonymous with "Good luck!" As advice, it certainly applies to fighting a fish, and it works in most artificial lure situations. But there are times, particularly when still-fishing with bait, when tight lines can cost you fish.

I enjoy all types of fishing. I troll, cast, flip, jerk, and drift. Not all at the same time, of course, although sometimes all in the same day. But there are situations when still-fishing with bait beats a more active approach. While few things are simpler and more relaxing than bait fishing, there is a lot more to it than just plunking a worm in a likely location.

For steelheaders, a stationary bait presentation is just the ticket in certain situations. In the spring, fall, and early winter months, the stream mouths, piers, and harbor areas are dotted with anglers, most of them still-fishing.

Most of these anglers use a slip sinker with a floating roe bag. (I often do well with an injected worm, too. But don't tell anyone.) They heave out their offering and slip their rods into a holder or prop them on a stick or rock. And they wait. While waiting for a bite they might chat with a buddy, sip some coffee, answer a call of nature, or admire a passing flock of geese. Steelhead seem to have a sixth sense for when we're distracted, selecting that exact moment to pick up the bait.

Sometimes the angler reacts in time and the battle is on. Sometimes the fish feels the pressure of the flailing rod and drops the bait. And on at least a dozen occasions over the years, I've seen a hapless angler's rod and reel go skittering into the water. (Remarkably, on one of those occasions another angler hooked the outfit within minutes of its loss and re-

---

NOT-SO-TALL TALE

Impressing the Boss

My fishing column in the local newspaper had given me a very modest level of local celebrity. My wife's boss told her he'd like to go out rainbow fishing with me sometime. I called him, and we arranged an outing.

He picked me up early, and we drove to the same dead-end dirt road that my brother-in-law Ken and I went to on our night-fishing excursion, described in the Bonanza and Beauty sidebar on pages 84–85.

It was late November and quite cold, the temperature hovering just above freezing. It started out just gray and dreary, but soon a light drizzle began to fall. We spent three or four fruitless and increasingly uncomfortable hours fishing the creek and the creek mouth. I had one hit in the lake itself, when I was drifting my float from the outflow of the creek. The fish jumped once, a beauty of about 10 pounds, but it threw the hook almost immediately afterward.

I was disappointed, not for myself, but for my wife's boss. He was a pleasant man and

had started the day chattering excitedly. Now only our teeth were chattering as we soddenly trudged back to the car.

The car that was covered in a layer of ice. The car that was parked on a road covered in a layer of ice. A road that negotiated two fairly large hills before intersecting with a well-traveled highway that the county would have salted by now.

The boss and I chipped the ice off the car. It was parked on a small rise, which we hoped would give us enough momentum to make it to the top of the next hill.

It didn't.

We made it about two-thirds of the way, and then, tires spinning and whining, slowly slid back to the bottom of the hill.

No one else was on the road. Nor could we expect anyone in the foreseeable future. And in those days, cell phones still seemed like something you might see on *Star Trek.* It was still drizzling, and the rain was freezing on contact.

The boss took a small shovel from the trunk, and I grabbed a tire iron. Together we slid and slashed our way up the hill, scoring turned it to its owner, who then managed to land the 5-pound steelie that was still attached. I wouldn't count on this happening, though.)

There are a few ways to avoid this occurrence. One is to hold your rod at all times. When the temperature is 38°F and the wind is knifing through every gap in your clothing, this is no darn fun. Your fingers would be happier in your pockets or wrapped around a coffee mug.

There are two ways to keep your bail open while preventing your line from spilling out—and your fingers from falling off. The most common

the ice surface, hoping to provide enough traction for the car to make it up. This time we wouldn't have the slight advantage of starting on a small rise. We cleared the area under the tires as best we could to provide some initial grip.

The boss got behind the wheel, and I got behind the car. He gunned the engine. I pushed. The car shot forward, and I fell face first. I was scrambling to my feet when I saw the car sliding back toward me, having not *quite* made it to the crest of the hill.

I rolled out of harm's way as the car came to rest in its former spot.

We made a couple half-hearted jokes before saving our breath for the next assault on the ice. It was laborious work under nasty circumstances. Had we been old friends, we might have turned it into a hysterically funny situation. But we'd only met hours ago. He was my wife's boss. The comedy was hard to find.

We agreed that if he made it to the top of the hill, he would just keep going until he crested the next (and last) one, where he could stop to wait for me.

After chipping, slashing, and swearing (the last on my part . . . the boss was a devout man), we were ready for another attempt.

He gunned. I pushed. I didn't fall. I watched him inch his way to the top of the hill . . . and . . . and . . . over!

I trudged to the crest, feeling almost happy until I saw the car resting at the bottom. He hadn't made it over the next one.

More chopping, slashing, and scoring. Much more muttered swearing. We were both worn out. My arms felt like lead, and I'm sure his were the same. We were both soaked and cold despite the work we were doing. As a bonus, I was covered in mud and still feeling the sting of pebbles churned back at me from the tires as I pushed.

We eventually made it out, of course. But it took hours. The drive home was pretty quiet. When he dropped me off, he bravely suggested we try this again some time, perhaps on a nicer day.

It never happened. But I have a hunch that this particular outing found a permanent home in his memory banks, too. ◀━

method is to make your cast, set your rod in a forked stick, open your bail, take out a bit of line, and anchor it with a small stone. The other approach is to wrap a small elastic band in front of your reel seat and loop a bit of line under it after opening your bail.

Neither of these practices is new—they've been used by anglers for ages. A mistake that many make, though, is to rely too heavily on their stone or their elastic, allowing their attentions to wander. The main reason for using these "line stoppers" is to prevent the current and/or wind from carrying your line away from the open bail. A secondary purpose, and well down the list for me, is as a bite indicator that buys you time if you are momentarily distracted.

I *always* allow a fair amount of slack—usually several feet—to hang from my rod tip after I cast and before anchoring with the stone. The wind and/or current forms an arc in the slack line that I watch like a hawk. This arc of slack line transmits the slightest unnatural movement. By watching it constantly, I can react instantly to any twitch or tightening of the slack. I remove the rock, or pull the line from the elastic, pick up the rod, and close the bail. In seconds, I'm ready for battle.

Many anglers keep their lines tight, even if using a stopper on an opened bail. Often, their first indication of a pickup is a throbbing rod tip, followed by line sizzling out from the stopper. Unfortunately, the fish feel this momentary resistance too, and often drop the bait before the angler can pick up his rod. Sometimes the angler is quick. Sometimes the fish hooks itself. I don't want to test those odds. By keeping a fair bit of slack in my line, I usually have time to spill my coffee and scramble to my feet before the line gets to the stopper.

I live in southern Ontario and often fish for steelhead during November and December gales. Dealing with extremes of wind and/or current can be difficult. You can minimize the effect of extreme winds by keeping your rod tip low, parallel to the water. An arc of just a few inches is better than none at all and will add a critical second or two to your reaction time. A strong current is best dealt with by keeping the rod tip high to minimize the amount of line in the water. If dealing with strong wind *and* strong current, you'll have to experiment to find a reasonably comfortable halfway point.

A pair of quality polarized sunglasses is a tremendous aid. They make "twitch-watching" infinitely easier, even when low-visibility mono is being used.

You can't always count on having a handy selection of stones available at your fishing spot, so I also carry a selection of pebbles of various sizes and weights in my vest or coat pocket. I use the lightest stone that conditions allow.

It doesn't matter whether you're fishing for steelhead, catfish, or carp, when utilizing the Do-Nothing method of bait fishing, keeping your line slack will lead to more "tight lines" when it counts.

Fillet Strips

I mentioned earlier that I occasionally kill a small perch to use as bait. I started doing this while fishing the weed-choked lake near my home. The two main angling tactics we use on this lake are casting with Erie Dearies or dunking jigs. We usually add a worm to the Dearie or a piece of one to the jig. Between nips by panfish (often perch) and tearing through the weeds, the worms sometimes don't last long. One day, as I unhooked one of the small perch that had managed to find the barb, I remembered my first decent bass.

I was about seven years old, and my father and I were out in a rowboat on a lake where we were renting a cottage. We'd run out of worms while catching panfish, catfish, and the occasional small bass. Dad killed and cut up a small perch. I affixed the tail section to my hook and cast it out. A few minutes later I had a bite. A few heart-throbbing moments after that, we were admiring a 15-inch smallmouth, by far my biggest fish up to that time.

Back to the future. I killed the small perch and filleted it. I then cut each small fillet lengthwise until I had six thin strips of flesh, skin still intact on one side. I affixed a strip to my Dearie and began fishing. The first advantage was that the panfish would peck at it but couldn't tear if off the hook. The second was that it stayed intact while it was being tugged through the weeds.

But It Seemed Like a Good Idea . . .

I n my midtwenties I was consumed with fishing. Having fun was a close second, but they often intertwined.

One night in early April, Ken and I sat around drinking coffee and yakking far into the night. Winter's grip had broken, and rainbows had been stampeding to their spawning grounds in the last few days. The season opener was still a couple of weeks away.

We got to talking about my family's cottage and a nearby speckled trout lake. The trout season was open up there. The recent stretch of decent weather should have rendered the last few miles of one-lane dirt road passable.

By 2 A.M. we were on the road. The last few miles, though a bit treacherous, were still negotiable. A little after 4:30 A.M., we were stumbling along the quarter-mile path through the woods that led to the lake. There was a little light from the quarter moon and stars. We might have wished it were a tad warmer than the high 30s Fahrenheit, but you can't have everything.

Worms weren't available at that time of year, so we rigged up with the only bait we had, roe bags, and fired them out. We leaned the rods on a nearby log and set about making a fire.

It was still a couple hours until dawn, so we made ourselves comfortable near the fire. Too comfortable, I suppose, because we both dozed off.

I awoke to Ken's hoots of laughter. He was holding his sides, unable to talk, and finally just pointed to the lake. Blinking against the unexpected daylight, I shaded my eyes and soon was doubled over myself, convulsing with laughter.

There, about 20 yards out from our rods, were our two neatly tied orange roe bags, resting a few feet apart from each other—on top of the ice.

Except for a couple of feet around the shoreline, the lake was still frozen over. I longed for a camera, but as with most of life's great moments, I had to settle for a mental picture.

We packed up and returned to the car, still chuckling. We navigated our way to the cottage, stoked the fireplace, found a tin of something to eat, and rested before heading home.

Sometimes the best fishing tales don't have a single fin involved. ◄◄

The third was a 4-pound walleye. We then decided to add a strip to the jig-grub combos we used.

Many more walleye, muskie, and even a few bass added proof to the pudding. Each strip would last an average of a couple of hours or so. Besides durability, I believe an added bonus was their strong scent, which was also a familiar one to other fish. Usually, we need to kill only one perch per trip, and sometimes we don't bother at all when we're getting satisfactory results with worms or grubs alone. But that 2-pound smallmouth from long ago added a very useful tool to the arsenal.

Thanks, Dad.

Drift-Casting for Salmon

As you know by now, I live near the shores of Lake Ontario. Over the last twenty years or so, all of the Great Lakes have experienced a boom in their fisheries, kick-started with the introduction of salmon. Various areas have boosted the fortunes of local anglers with increased stockings of rainbow, brown, and lake trout, as well as the salmon. Since these fish don't exactly respect boundaries, except at spawning time, Ontario anglers benefit from New York fish and vice versa. Anglers fortunate enough to have large, well-equipped boats, or those who hire one of the many knowledgeable charter-boat operators, benefit the most during the summer months. Since the schools of fish are often found across many miles of open water, the shore bound or small-boat angler must wait until early spring to have a go at steel-head or until fall for a shot at salmon, browns, steelies again, and lakers.

It's at or around spawning time, though, that the fish begin to stage outside their home creeks or rivers. This gives everyone a chance to get in on the act: pier or shore anglers, small-boat operators, as well as the big boys. This used to lead to chaotic scenes, as 12-foot aluminum boats trolled within a hundred feet of 28-foot charter boats—all not far outside the casting range of pier fishermen.

Those scenes are rare now in many areas of the Great Lakes, largely because of the accidental introduction of a tiny, but prolific creature: the zebra mussel. A native of Asia, the zebra mussel was first noted on our side of the pond in 1988 in Lake Saint Clair, near Detroit. It most likely was introduced via discharged bilgewater from an ocean-liner or freighter. It quickly spread throughout the Great Lakes, south through a good portion of the eastern-central U.S., and into inland waterways in Ontario and Québec.

The zebra mussel is a filter feeder, extracting microscopic particles from the water. They live in huge clusters, affixing themselves to rocks, water pipes, and boat hulls. The most visible sign of their presence is the gin-clear water that results from their filtering. In the area I fish, on calm days, bottom is clearly visible 20 feet down. This increased visibility makes fish skittish and fishing for them more difficult. Even salmon, driven by the urge to spawn and scenting the incoming water of their natal streams, are reluctant to gather at the mouths during high light penetration days. They will move up at night or wait for a decent rain to cloud the outflow area, masking their passage.

As a result, anglers have had to change their tactics. Pier fishermen have tried lighter lines or night fishing. The larger boats work deeper water, well past the time of year when they would usually find the fish in closer. Smaller craft have to troll with extra long lines out, hoping that the fish spooked by the motor will have regrouped by the time the lure goes by. Having a hundred yards of line trailing the boat makes weaving through traffic a nightmare and hook-sets problematic.

A solution that often works for us is not to troll at all. It must be a form of heresy to abandon trolling because I have seen very few anglers copy us. We will drift and cast lures—usually plugs, sometimes spoons—near creek outflows. This quieter approach, coupled with relatively light 8-pound line, has allowed us to lock horns with chinook, steelhead, and coho, with the occasional bonus bass and brown trout thrown in. It's a tremendous thrill to have a 30-pound chinook strike your lure only 15 feet from the boat.

The best days for this type of fishing are overcast, after a rain, and with a light chop. Since I only have a 14-foot boat, those 5-foot rollers, which can be

KARL BARON

Most of the Author shown with all of a nice chinook salmon caught while drifting and casting in the harbor of a Great Lakes tributary.

common, keep me shore-bound. Even bobbing atop 2- or 3-footers can make casting uncomfortable. The overall best lure the last couple of years has been Cotton Cordell's Rattlin' Spot or variations. It casts like a bullet, sinks quickly (unless using the suspending models), and can be retrieved at a high, annoying-to-salmon speed. The hooks, and the lure itself, are strong, as they must be to survive a walloping from these beasties.

I use an 8-foot medium-action rod with a large reel that holds over 300 yards of 8-pound test line. The extra foot of rod helps when wrestling a large fish yet isn't so long that casting is difficult.

The bait-fishing tactics used by the pier anglers can be successful from a boat as well, though calm days are better for this approach. A drifted egg sinker quickly collects algae in late summer and early fall in these parts. And we don't use an anchor because we might have to start the motor quickly to chase after one of these finned fullbacks.

If you're one of the millions of anglers ringing the Great Lakes who thinks bait fishing, casting from piers, or trolling are the only ways to catch salmon and trout, give drift-casting a try. You're in for a real treat.

In-Between Steelhead

This section is more about an often overlooked and underfished type of water in the Great Lakes area than it is about a special angling technique. In late fall and early winter, most fishermen concentrate their efforts on harbor or breakwall areas or in places farthest upstream (on sections of streams with year-round angling).

There are times, however, when lots of fish and few anglers are in between these areas.

Over the years I've learned that there are a couple distinct types of steelheaders. Some anglers find a comfortable spot on a pier or breakwall, hunker down, fire out a slip-sinker rigged roe bag, and wait for the fish. These anglers get their share of action too, primarily when the fish are staging during spring and early through late fall. Many of these anglers are old-timers, whose best stream-tramping days are behind them. Some, like me at times, simply enjoy this relaxed approach to fishing for steelies.

Another breed, generally younger, prefers to fish faster upstream water. Getting "numb bum" from parking themselves on a rock for hours is not for them. They like to cover water, seeking the fish in a variety of holes and using different presentations. I am among their ranks too, usually after spring or fall rains have discolored and raised the water, calling the fish in from the mouths of the streams. Depending on the time of year, water depth, and available cover, these fish may hang around for some time. But, inevitably, the water level drops, the fish become spooky, and, particularly in the fall, they drop back down toward the harbor areas.

Some return all the way to the big water, giving the breakwall crew a little more action. Some don't. In fact, the last nice November rain that sent quite a few fish up into the faster water didn't lure all of them. Many fall-run steelhead, not completely driven by the spawning urge, only poke their noses into a stream or river after a rain. They leave the relative safety of open water to travel a short distance upstream, but often stop for prolonged periods in the deeper, slower water not far from the mouth.

This is where I catch a lot of them.

Slow-moving, featureless stretches of water sometimes provide wonderful angling—if you time it right.

This water typically has a slow current, and the surrounding land can be marshy. In fact, some waterways branch off and form small bays. Marinas are often found smackdab in the middle of these sections, and as long as the weather is nice (ugh), boat traffic can sometimes be a headache. At a glance, the water looks featureless. The only visible structure might be overhanging tree limbs, docks, or bends in the waterway. It's not glamorous water; in fact, it can be downright homely.

But to my mind, this type of water offers the best of both breakwall and upstream angling. Although the pools aren't as distinct as they are upstream, an angler can still walk and cover water. The long, deep, slow runs are custom-made for float-fishing. I generally use dime- or nickel-sized roe bags or small worms fished on a 4- to 6-pound leader attached to an 8-pound main line. On dirty days, when the water is high and/or discolored, I'll just use the 8-pound line. My rod length varies from 9 to 13 feet. I'll use the shorter rod if I intend to toss a few spinners, spoons, or plugs, an approach that can also pay dividends for these in-between fish. I will not, of course, use the light leader when casting lures.

This water also lends itself well to the Do-Nothing approach. I will often park at a likely looking spot and toss out a floating worm or roe bag and then wait. This method is most effective in the deepest, slowest areas, especially during particularly frigid days, when both fish and anglers are sluggish. While the harbor crew usually uses $1/2$-ounce or heavier sinkers for casting distance and to combat wind and waves, it is rarely necessary to use more than $1/8$-ounce sinkers in the lower portions of tributary rivers. In fact, unless a long cast is called for, I usually just use a single shot sinker, which adds weight but stays light enough to tumble slowly along bottom with the current.

The slower current usually associated with these areas exhibits a unique "back and forth" tendency. Although the current flows toward the harbor mouth over most of its course, it will, with varying degrees of regularity, slow, pause completely, or even reverse itself for a while. There are days, particularly when the outflowing current is quite strong, when most of my hits or pickups occur during the pause phase. The only theory I have to account for this is that the fish hold their positions when the current flows, expending as little energy as possible. When it pauses, they can more easily roam about and investigate food sources.

If you want to intercept spring-run steelhead in these in-between waters, timing is critical. Once the ice has melted and the water warms slightly, they leave their staging areas and move upstream to spawning water. Because the current is usually sluggish and holes may not be clearly defined, there is nothing to slow their upstream progress. They will only remain in these areas longer if the water level drops and clears precipitously.

It is a *much* different story in the fall and winter, however. I have caught trout with some consistency in these waters from October through February as long as there is open, unfrozen water. As most avid steelhead anglers know only too well, the best days are often the least comfortable. Cold, dark, rainy, or snowy days with windchills that turn your fingers into disobedient lumps seem to be the days that offer the best chance of success.

Fall-run steelhead are like a nervous bride and groom on their wedding night: eager but edgy. They will charge upstream when a decent rain swells the water, hover for a day or two, and then, when the water clears and lowers, they quickly drop back. Usually, though, not all of them drop all the way back to the lake. They will often park for days or weeks in these in-between areas, waiting for the right circumstances to move upstream again.

The vast majority of these fish are not spawners, although last year I did catch two very ripe females. Some of these fish may be following salmon and browns to scoop up caviar, but I think most are just a little confused and excited by fall rains and temperatures, which so closely mirror spring conditions.

I don't, however, spend a whole lot of time wondering *why* they are there. I just happily watch my drifting float or sit on the bank and sip my coffee while waiting for my line to twitch. I am thankful that they *are* there, and will be from fall to freeze-up.

▶ **Although these waters are largely devoid of trout and salmon from late spring to early fall, they are not devoid of fish. Pike, carp, bass, catfish, silver bass, and assorted panfish are there for the catching. These sections of the creeks and rivers are often great places to take kids in the off season. Pack a lunch and take some folding lawn chairs. The panfish will keep the kids busy, and you just might be called upon to help wrestle a 20-pound carp. As a bonus, the surrounding marshlands often make for some great bird-watching.**

CHAPTER *10*

Tips, Tricks, and Odds and Ends

Paying Attention

If you want to catch fish more consistently (and who doesn't?), there's one simple thing you can do. Every time you catch a decent fish, ask yourself *why* you caught it. Why did that fish hit? Where was my lure and at what speed was it being retrieved? How deep was it? Was it near structure? If so, what type? Note the wind direction and time of day. Triangulate your position and note where you were when the fish hit.

By doing this consistently (keep a notebook if you like), you'll eventually establish patterns for certain times of year on certain bodies of water. And patterns are the key to consistent success.

The Wind Is Our Friend

Fishing the leeward, or calm, side of a body of water may be more comfortable, but chances are the fish are waving to you from the other side, especially if the wind direction has been consistent for a couple of days.

In lakes, wind moves plankton and other tiny goodies, which can stack up on shorelines or structure facing the wind. Little fish follow these goodies and big fish follow the little fish. Get in line if you want in on the action.

Money-Saving Knot

You'll eventually need to learn more than just the knot for connecting your terminal tackle (lure to line). A Blood Knot is used to connect two pieces of monofilament of similar diameter. Learning to tie one properly takes patience, but mastering it can save you time and money.

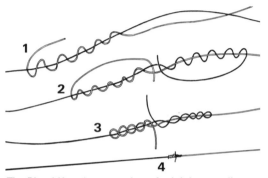

The Blood Knot is a great knot for joining two lines of similar diameter. This knot is tricky to tie, but it will save you money and fish. **1.** Overlap lines and turn one end around the other five or so times. Pinch first loop between thumb and forefinger and repeat the step with the other tag end. **2.** Push one tag end up through the original loop and the other tag end down through it. **3.** Holding tag ends tightly, slowly draw the knot tight. **4.** Trim tag ends.

Most medium-sized spinning reels hold in excess of 200 yards of 8-pound test line. Most fishing situations, however, call for much less. Repeatedly cutting frayed line, break-offs due to snags, and so on will sooner or later cost you 20 to 80 yards of line and make longer casts impossible.

Instead of stripping off all the line to change it, just strip off a few more yards and use a Blood Knot to attach new monofilament to your existing line. It's rare that a large fish will strip a hundred yards of line on a run, but it happens, and a properly tied Blood Knot will stand the test.

Set that Hook!

The most common error I see among rookie anglers is improperly setting the hook. Many don't set it at all—they simply continue to reel in when a fish hits. Most of these fish never learn what the inside of a boat looks like.

Most good hook-sets are accomplished with a sharp upward sweep of the rod. Because monofilament has elastic properties, it is virtually impossible to set the hook hard enough to break the line or rod. Yes, I said "virtually." There are exceptions, of course, such as when you have very little line out and your "fish" is really an underwater, immovable object. You also needn't "slam it" if fishing for smaller fish.

In most instances, however, you cannot set the hook *too* hard.

If you are still-fishing, using live-bait rigs, or drifting with a float, close your bail before setting the hook. Wait for the moving fish to tighten your slack line or retrieve it by reeling slowly. Just before putting the boots to the fish, wrap one finger around the line, near the reel, so that there is *no* drag release when you set the hook.

If you're casting and retrieving lures and a fish hits, you won't have time for the finger-wrapping move, so make sure your drag is set properly before you start.

Often, the worst thing that can happen if you set the hook too hard is whiffing completely. Be alert and prepared to duck quickly if this happens. I shattered an eyeglass lens once when a sinker came back to me at the speed of light.

Drag Adjustment

This brings us to proper drag adjustment. On spinning reels, the drag is an adjustable knob or thingamajig located at the front of the spool, the back of the reel, or the bottom of the reel. Many are numbered and have "click-stop" positions. I prefer the variety that does not have click-stops because it allows for finer tuning.

The tighter the drag is set, the more resistance the fish feels when fighting.

▶ **Never set your drag higher than the breaking strength of your line.**

If your drag is set too tightly, either your line or your rod will break if you set the hook into a large fish or an immovable snag.

Experience is the only teacher when it comes to proper drag adjustment. I usually fish with my drag set at about half the breaking point of my line. I will tighten it more if casting and retrieving lures.

If you set the hook and the drag immediately releases on a small or middling fish, you've set it too loosely. If a big fish wants to go and your drag says no, you've set it too tightly.

Your drag's main purpose is to allow a good fish to run and to tire it out while not overly stressing your line. Drag tension does not remain constant.

It can vary depending on how much line is out, how long you've been fishing, or whether you've already fought a fish or two. Get into the habit of checking it frequently, at least every 15 minutes or so during active fishing.

Test your drag by simply closing the bail and pulling the line straight out from the reel with your free hand. It should come out smoothly but grudgingly. You'll soon develop the proper feel for it.

Another common beginner mistake, particularly with that first really big fish, is to reel in constantly, even when the drag is releasing. Most drags make an audible (and oh-so-sweet) sound when they are operating.

▶ **Never reel in when your drag is releasing line.**

Not only will you not gain an inch by reeling in, but if you continue to do so you'll twist your line into an un-fishable mess—as you'll discover on the next cast you attempt. When a fish is taking out line, just hold your rod high and let the pressure of the rod and drag tire it out. Sometimes, with a very big fish, you may have to chase after it, retrieving slackened line as you go. But as soon as you reestablish tight contact, stop reeling and let your drag work for you.

When a big fish pauses after a run, "pump" it to regain lost line and to keep the fish from resting too long. Lift your rod high, then reel in while dropping the tip. Stop reeling and lift up again, then reel back down. Keep repeating this pumping process until you start winning the battle. If the fish goes on a fresh run, let him. When he stops, pump again.

Proper drag adjustment is what allows us to land 30-pound fish on 6- to 8-pound line.

That, and room to run . . . and no snags . . . and a proper hookset . . . and luck . . . and Venus being aligned with Mars . . . and Murphy looking the other way.

The Anti-Reverse

There's another little do-hickey on your reel. It's a little button or lever that turns the anti-reverse on or off. When the anti-reverse is on, the reel handle can only be turned forward. When it's off, the reel handle can be turned backward, as well.

Who would want the reel handle to turn backward? If you have less than a couple of thousand hours on the water, *not* you.

Keeping the anti-reverse on prevents most backlashes or "bird nests," those alarming tangles of line that can be a misery to unravel. If you try to test your drag with the anti-reverse off, the reel will spin merrily backward, line will uncoil, and your drag will not come into play. In almost every conceivable fishing situation, you want the anti-reverse *on*.

Here comes the exception.

About thirty years ago, I tangled with my first chinook salmon. I was casting a spinner in the lower end of a river, near the lake mouth. It hit. I set the hook. It took off. My drag screamed, then seized up completely. My line popped. Ten seconds after that fish hit I was looking at a ruined reel with puffs of smoke coming from it.

Since then, I have never *completely* trusted a drag, no matter how expensive the reel or how smoothly the drag appears to be operating.

When I fight a large fish these days I turn off my anti-reverse, particularly when the fish is near the boat or bank. Rather than put all my faith in my drag, I back-reel when the fish decides it wants to go again or when it makes a sudden change in direction. As long as I keep my hand on the handle, the drag does its job. My back-reeling is more insurance against the possibility of the drag not releasing initially when that large fish takes off.

In every other fishing situation I can think of, though, the anti-reverse should be left on.

Check that Action

Another common mistake inexperienced anglers make is failing to check the speed of their lures, particularly when trolling. Always run your lure beside the boat to see how it's operating before heaving it out. Trolling too fast or slow for the lure you are using can lead to a skunking.

Don't assume that the same speed you are using for a spinner will be right for a plug. Always check when changing lures. Often, you'll have the speed down perfectly when trolling into the wind, but may have to make an adjustment when you turn with the wind.

Line, the All-Important Connector

Some of the new "super" lines on the market, like Spider Wire, have little or no stretch. Their main advantages over mono are their thinner diameters and their ability to transmit the slightest tick and twitch to the alert angler. I confess to not having a lot of hands-on experience with these lines.

I like the idea of improved "feel," but the stretching qualities of mono make it more forgiving of mistakes and quick hits from big, close-range fish.

I can see using these lines in deep-water, long-line situations where the improved feel would come in handy. The long-range hook-set in these situations would also lessen the possibility of breaking the rod tip on a big fish or a snag.

Using 30-pound line with the diameter of 8-pound mono is also appealing when it comes to chasing big muskie or pike. Many muskie maniacs and bass anglers who work heavy cover use lines rated as high as 65 pounds. Proper drag adjustment would be absolutely critical, though. If your drag doesn't release, something else has to give, and it just might be your rod.

These newer lines are much more expensive than good mono, and to date their cost and limitations in some situations pose no threat to monofilament's position as the all-around line of choice for most fishermen.

Whatever line you use, check it frequently for fraying. The tiniest nick will weaken your line considerably, leading to lost fish (usually the fish you least want to lose). After every snag and every fish landed or lost, run your fingers lightly up from the knot at your lure for several feet. If you feel the slightest nick, cut your line above that point and reattach your lure.

You'll thank me one day.

A Pause Can Aid the Cause

Just because a lure is designed to be fished on a straight retrieve—like spinners, spoons, and most plugs—doesn't mean it always should be.

▶ **An occasional pause during the retrieve often triggers a strike from a following fish.**

This little trick has worked many times for me.

Quite often, a lure will attract a fish's attention, but its relative "strangeness" dictates caution. The fish follows the lure out of curiosity, but often shies away rather than commit to a strike. A short pause once or twice during a retrieve causes the lure to stop, or flutter downward in the case of sinking lures. This sudden appearance of "weakness" is irresistible to many reluctant fish. On some days, half my hits come on the pause.

This has occurred many times when I'm casting heavy spoons from breakwalls or piers, primarily for rainbows. Unlike most strikes, when an angler feels a sharp jerk or an abrupt stoppage, hits by following fish are barely felt. They are indicated by a sudden *slackening* of line as the charging fish continues on *toward* you. Until you begin to anticipate it, it's an odd feeling to have to retrieve line like a madman until it's tight enough to set the hook.

Pausing a drifting bait can also pay dividends at times. Sometimes good fish will hold at the bottom end of a pool. Drifted bait, particularly under a float, only remains in the "zone" for a few seconds before drifting out. If repeated drifts don't encourage a hit, I will often "check," or stop, my drift when it reaches the prime area. Often, a fish that had no difficulty ignoring the moving bait will smack the one that refuses to go away.

Incorporating the "pause" into your retrieves will add a few fish to your tally that otherwise may never have hit.

Bumpers, Nudgers, and Short-Strikers

On some days it seems that the fish are hitting "short." You are feeling bumps and small hits but aren't making contact. If you're using lures, try downsizing a little or adding bait or a drop of scent.

Sometimes these near-hits represent wishful thinking by small panfish. Often, though, I believe they are half-hearted, exploratory nudges from neutral or negative fish. The addition of bait or scent helps to convince them that your offering is worth a more determined approach. If they've recently fed, a smaller tidbit may be more appealing than another main course.

But if you downsize and/or add bait and are still not making contact, consider adding a "stinger." A stinger is another hook, usually a single, that you attach to the rearmost hook of your lure.

The easiest way to add a stinger is to make sure the hook eye is large enough to slide over the barb of your main hook. You can squeeze down the barb of your main hook with pliers to make it easier. Some jigs are sold with stingers already in place.

After you slide on the stinger, it can be kept from flopping around by forcing a small piece of elastic band over and past the barb of the main hook. Sometimes, particularly when using jigs or spinners, the addition of a stinger will nab those short-strikers.

STINGER HOOK

A "stinger" hook attached to a spinner or jig is an ideal setup for tagging fish that strike short.

Hook Hones

A good hook hone or sharpener is essential. There are a lot of models available, from modestly priced small stones to expensive diamond-edged or battery-powered sharpeners. I like smaller stones that are grooved on one side. They are light, easy to use, affordable, and don't take up a lot of space.

Most quality single hooks are sticky-sharp right from the package, and most lure hooks are sharper than they were a few years ago. But some lure hooks need a touch-up from a hone before hitting the water. *Any* hook should be checked after landing a fish or two or after encountering a snag. I've seen many anglers lose successive fish and never check to see if the hook is sharp. A dull hook is often the culprit when you fail to make contact with a willing fish.

The Pike

My brother Karl once had an interesting encounter with a giant pike while fishing at our cottage lake. He and Dad were drifting for walleyes. Karl had hooked a 2-pounder and had reeled it in until it was directly below the boat. A few more feet and it would be landed. But it suddenly stopped dead and began moving away quickly. His drag sang, and he knew by the huge increase in weight and power that a giant pike must have grabbed the walleye and moved off. A few seconds later he reeled in a broken line.

At that time we'd had our cottage for over thirty years. During those years the largest pike we'd caught was a 12-pounder, and that was twenty years ago (I'm blushing modestly here). I don't believe anyone in the family had even been close to double-digits before or since. There are not a lot of pike in the lake, and we only catch a handful a year. The average is probably 4 pounds or so, with 6- to 7-pounders meriting special attention.

So the story of the one that grabbed Karl's walleye had everyone buzzing. He estimated it ran at least 20 pounds.

About a week later I was at the cottage and fishing in the same area, our favorite spot for walleye. I'd taken a couple of decent fish and a couple of small ones. I was reeling in what felt like another 17-incher when it suddenly stopped. It's a rocky area, and it was not uncommon for a hooked fish to jam the sinker, or itself, between a couple of rocks. When that happens, our only option is to start the motor and move to the other side of the obstruction.

I was reaching for the motor when my line began moving out at an unhurried pace. My drag hummed. I was puzzled for a second, as 17-inchers don't usually do this. Finally, my 15-watt bulb went off, and I realized that I was attached to Karl's pike. I knew I had little chance of landing it, but I was at least hoping for a glimpse. Alas, my encounter only lasted a few more seconds before my hook pulled free from that poor doomed walleye. But it was long enough to know I'd never encountered a fish near that size in our lake before. It was big enough to start my imagination racing at what might be happening down there. And, of course, it was big enough to make reeling in a walleye even more exciting.

By the way, I'm a few years older than Karl. Many of those years were spent on the water, so my Heightened Awareness is a bit further along than his. I put that pike at 25 pounds. ⬤◀

Protect Yourself

I always have some sunscreen and bug repellent in my bag, for obvious reasons. The incidence of skin cancer among fishermen is alarmingly high. Baseball-style caps don't protect the ears and neck. Get a wide-brimmed hat and wear sunscreen on those bright days.

The most effective repellents are those with a relatively high concentration of DEET, the short form of an unpronounceable string of chemical names (for the terminally curious: N,N-diethyl-meta-toluamide). Children and those with sensitive skin should use lower concentrations. DEET can damage some plastics, including monofilament, so don't splash it around willy-nilly. I've heard claims regarding the bug-repelling properties of some pleasant-smelling skin lotions, but my own field tests found that bugs weren't deterred in the least. Stick to DEET if you're in heavily infested areas. Light-colored clothing is also less apt to attract flying beasties than dark-colored clothing.

In Case of Accidents

A first-aid kit is one of those items you may never need for years but one day will be happy you packed. At the very least, you should carry a few bandages and pain tablets in a waterproof container.

A roll of electrical tape, duct tape, or other waterproof tape can come in handy for emergency repairs. I also use it to more firmly anchor my reels to rods with sliding reel seats. A tube of instant glue is also handy for emergency repairs, and a drop of it can be used to anchor the head of a plastic grub to the backside of a jig head.

Handy Bags

I always carry a few plastic bags with me. Smallish, zippered bags are excellent for storing loose roe. Larger, grocery-type bags are handy for separating your lunch from your bait, carrying small fish, and for collecting garbage. Garbage bags are good for transporting larger catches, keeping your caboose dry on wet ground or rocks, and for making emergency rain vests when you stupidly leave your rain gear behind.

This, of course, has never happened to me.

Keeping Bait Healthy

Keep your bait fresh, which usually means "cool." When boat fishing, always keep worms in a cooler. If using minnows, keep them in one of those floating buckets tied to the boat. If you don't have one, use a regular bucket and change the water frequently.

In the field, find a shady spot for your bait. Putting an ice cube or two over shredded newspaper that covers your worms can help. Use white bait containers, which reflect sunlight. Amazingly, though, I've found they don't stay white for long.

When using roe, take only as many as you may need for that day. For me, this means a minimum of 60 bags. Optimism + Boy Scout Syndrome = Prepared For The Best Day Of My Life. If you're less optimistic, 20 might do.

Every avid trout or salmon angler has a favorite method for curing roe for long-term storage. Here's one simple, inexpensive, and proven method.

First, make sure you do an initial field rinse. Immediately after procuring the loose roe (but *after* reviving and releasing the female), put the roe into one of those zippered plastic bags and add some creek or lake water. Slosh it around for two or three minutes, drain, and repeat. If the water is icy cold, the initial rinsing will probably be enough. This will harden the eggs slightly and retard spoilage until you get them home. This initial hardening is crucial. Without it the eggs soften rapidly and the rest of the curing process will not work at all, or not nearly as well.

As soon as you get home, place the roe in a quart or so of *cold* water, into which you have dissolved a few tablespoons of borax. Borax powder is available at pharmacies, or you can use 20 Mule Team Borax from the grocery store. Refrigerate the container for at least a few hours or up to a few days.

Some anglers like to divide the container into smaller compartments and experiment with food coloring or other dyes to alter the color of the eggs. If you have plenty, feel free to experiment. I've had good days with red and orange, but natural is a safe bet most days.

When you're ready to tie the roe into bags or when they've cured long enough, drain them through a colander or sieve and then let them air dry. Store cured eggs in an airtight bag or container in the fridge. With luck, they will keep for several weeks or even months. If they start to get a bit gamey (family members with more delicate sensibilities will alert you), soak them again in the water with borax.

If you have roe that's still encased in its skein, as can happen when you keep a female for the table, a different approach is called for. Using scissors (not a knife), cut the skeins into dime- or nickel-sized chunks. It's best to do this over several layers of newspapers. Let the chunks air dry for a few minutes.

In a plastic margarine container, sprinkle enough borax powder to coat the bottom. Add enough chunks of roe to make a single layer. Cover this layer with more borax. Repeat until all the chunks are covered. You can also add chunks to a plastic bag with borax in it. Make sure the pieces are well coated. Stored in the fridge, these eggs will last for months, but you may occasionally have to add a little more borax and shake them up.

There are basically two ways to affix your hook to the roe bags. Some people slip the hook just under the knot formed when tying the top of the bag closed, and others embed the hook completely in the bag itself. Either way works just fine.

CABELA'S INC.

A spawn-tying machine for making roe bags. Colored bits of Styrofoam are often enclosed to make the bags float.

Other Bait

Some of you may be scratching your heads by now, wondering why I never mentioned frogs, crayfish, or salamanders in my references to bait.

The answer is I just don't use them. They're too high up on the evolutionary ladder for me to feel comfortable killing or injuring them. These critters work well, though, and the first two are very popular baits. It's a judgment call each of us has to make, and I draw the line at worms, minnows, and leeches.

I've had decent results using scented plastic imitations of these critters, and that's good enough for me.

Scents Can Make Sense

As I've discussed throughout this book, adding bait (and its natural scent and taste) to a lure can improve success. And I am an enthusiastic convert to many of the new scented plastics. Some bottled scents supposedly attract specific species, and others claim to attract all species of fish.

Many anglers swear by the use of scent, but I only use it occasionally to add a drop to a scentless grub or to a lure. The only time I'm sure scent has increased my success is when I drift small bits of sponge (to simulate roe) in fast water while fishing for trout or salmon.

Scent actually may be more important in masking human odor than in attracting fish. Some studies have indicated that fish dislike a chemical secreted through human sweat called L-serine. Some folks may have a higher concentration of this chemical than others. This may partly account for why some anglers get skunked while nearby anglers using the same tackle and techniques whack fish after fish.

If you seem to be on the wrong side of that equation more often than not, scent may be worth a try. And if using scent makes you feel more confident about your presentation, that alone is a good enough reason.

CHAPTER 11

A New Euphemism

I began writing this book several years ago. Soon, I had a couple of spiral notebooks filled with longhand and rife with cross-outs and cramped additions in the margins. Instead of rewriting it on my typewriter, I caved in to the urgent pleadings of my oldest son and bought a computer.

I couldn't get my word-processing program to work despite weeks of wrestling with it, so the next version was written in Wordpad (like training wheels for a neophyte word-processor user). It looked terrible, but at least the book was taking shape. A stack of white paper with typewritten words on it more closely resembles a book than notebooks filled with scribbling.

One day, a miracle happened—my word-processing software worked—and I was able to revise and rewrite the manuscript. I found out later that My Kindly Editor hated this particular piece of software. A couple years went by. I hadn't spent *all* that time just laboring over the keyboard, however. I also did what every respectable writer does before embarking on a project.

I researched.

I researched creeks, rivers, ponds, and lakes. I researched trout, salmon, walleye, muskie, and most any other creature with fins. Some days, I researched from dawn to past dusk. I was a paragon of dedication.

When I was a young boy, I learned very early that when Dad said to Mom, "I think Stan and I are *getting away* Wednesday," what he meant was "going fishing." Other euphemisms were adopted over the years: "wet a line," "get some fresh air," "heading out." All of which implied an activity that was a break from the "real" day-to-day world of work and worry, one that was vaguely "wrong" somehow.

My new euphemism, however, not only had an air of dignity about it, but righteousness as well.

"Mr. Baron? It's Ms. Your-Son's-Teacher here. We need a couple parent volunteers to accompany the children to the Museum of Ceramic Shakespearean Characters tomorrow, and I was wondering if we could count on you?"

"Gee. That sounds like fun. Unfortunately, I've got hours of Research scheduled for tomorrow."

I learned early on how to pronounce the word with a capital R. It brooked little argument.

Oh, sure, I got a few raised eyebrows, nudges, and winks from family and friends. But mild ridicule is a tiny price to pay for justifying what you love to do.

Recent Research Results

The fall and winter of 2001–2002 was not a great one for steelhead in my part of the world. It was very dry, and water levels were low. The infrequent rain and snow were barely enough to color the water. The fish that did come up didn't hover very long. Even the few that remained in the lower, slower sections were spooky due to the water clarity.

I had the occasional decent day, and rarely went entirely fishless, but those fish did not come easily. One plus was that it was a mild winter; it was mid-January before the creeks froze over.

I spent the next month writing in earnest, and a mid-February thaw had mostly escaped my notice. Then Karl called from work one morning and said, "It's nice out. You should get out." I demurred, citing my own work, and settled back in front of the keyboard.

For about five minutes.

I got up to look out the window. Cloudy. Puddles from the melting snow. It *had* been a month since my last research session.

A half-hour later I was trundling along the well-worn path to my favorite section of the lower creek. The temperature was a downright balmy 40°F. The water looked decent, slightly off color, slightly high. There was only a little ice along the banks, which would disappear within hours. I rigged up with a float and roe bag on a 6-pound leader.

I'd seen one small boil at the surface while I was rigging up, but no sign of life since then.

I fell into a familiar rhythm. Cast upstream. Retrieve slack as the float drifts back toward me. Extend arm to the right to stretch the drift a bit longer. Reel in. Repeat.

Cast . . . drift . . . stretch . . . reel . . . repeat. The sequence took about a minute. I never took my eyes off the tiny float.

An hour passed. Then two. My shoulders began to ache, but I knew that would pass too, and it did. I never took my eyes off the tiny float. I was in a state of self-hypnosis that is probably familiar to some of you. The body is engaged in a routine, nearly mindless task, and the mind drifts free from its moorings. I thought about everything and nothing. Time didn't much matter. I never took my eyes off the tiny float. There was only the rhythm of the routine. The water that moved but stayed the same. The tiny float that was gone. The unhurried . . . huh?

I set the hook. The rhythm had broken. My 11-foot rod bent into that lovely arc, and my drag sang. I knew it was a beauty from the get-go. The fish didn't waste any energy on jumps. One swirl at the surface early on, though, confirmed what I'd already felt: A big 'bow.

After short runs upstream and down, we settled into a tug-of-war. The fish sulked about 20 yards out. I leaned on my rod. He didn't move, I didn't let up. I'd experienced this with salmon a couple of times before, but not with a steelie. After a few minutes of this nonnegotiating, I walked downstream to alter the angle of my pressure.

It worked. He began to move, taking drag again then stopping. I pumped and retrieved and prodded him into action. It was far from a spectacular fight, but it was a long one.

About twenty minutes later I was admiring a beautiful male, easily 15 pounds and possibly a little more. He'd been in the creek long enough to acquire the crimson cheeks and slash down the sides.

He was a strong, healthy fish, and I only had to hold him in the water for a few seconds before he swam off.

I'd caught quite a few steelhead up to 12 pounds or so and had lost bigger fish over the years. But that surprise 'bow in mid-February was the largest I'd landed, and a wonderful example of how diligent research can pay off. And that sometimes it pays to listen to your younger brother.

I was immersed in work for most of the spring and summer. My research waned significantly. By the time August rolled around, I'd only been fishing twice since that February 'bow and had yet to visit the cottage. I was tired, stressed, and not a whole lot of fun to be around. Finally, I cleared my calendar in mid-August and went to the cottage for some much needed RR&R (rest, relaxation, and research).

It seemed I'd brought my black cloud with me, though. In the first five days my outboard broke down three times. I spent a lot more hours driving to and from the nearest repair shop than I did on the water. Except, of course, the hours I spent on the water waiting for someone to come along and tow me back to the cottage. (Thanks again, John!)

But the last five days of our summer vacation were problem free, and I finally got into my usual cottage frame of mind. I got up before dawn each day and fished until midmorning. The weather was warm and sunny, great for swimming, and the kids had a lot of fun. The fishing was only so-so. I got a few smallish walleye every morning and evening. And I caught my first pike ever on a floating worm. I was reasonably content.

My last full day was a Made-For-Fishing day. Dark and rainy. In fact, it poured for most of the day. I got a pair of nice 20-inch walleye in the morning and a few other smaller ones. I got my first decent smallie of the trip, a 2-pounder, followed shortly after by one that neared 3 pounds.

I went back in for breakfast and to change into dry clothes. My second foray out started during a welcome lull in the rain. I back-trolled with a floating jig head–worm combo and took two more nice walleye.

I decided to try casting a jig for a while. I tied on a black, $^3/_8$-ounce head and threaded on a 4-inch black grub. I was working the top of my favorite structure. Under the prevailing conditions the walleye had moved up into 13 feet of water.

Then the skies opened, and the rain returned with a vengeance. I could barely see. It was coming down in sheets and my glasses, despite the bill of my hat, were streaming with water. There was no way to see my line twitch. I thought my first cast would probably be my last before either packing it in or going back to trolling.

I didn't need to see the hit. I felt it just fine and set the hook into a solid fish. The water erupted off to my left with a resounding splash. I didn't see the fish itself, but the long, slashing wake it left behind seemed like that of a good pike or muskie.

There was one other fool (pardon me, dedicated angler) out there that morning. He was trolling slowly with his electric motor about 30 yards to my right. He'd heard the splash too, and turned to see my rod bend.

"That sounded *huge!*" he called out.

"Pike, I think," came my reply through gritted teeth.

The fish decided it wanted to go under the boat, and I slid, sprawled, and scrambled my way to the prow to try to avoid the motor. I stuck my rod down into the water and followed the fish to the other side. He didn't jump again, and after a couple of minutes of slugging it out, I began to work him closer to the surface.

The relatively short fight confirmed in my mind that I was dealing with a pike. I'd been lured into a false sense of security many times by this tactic, only to have the fish explode into another run at boatside.

So I was only toying with the idea of reaching for the net when I saw a thick, bronze, un-pike-like shape appear. It was a smallmouth bass. It was a *very* big smallmouth bass.

A moment later my net bulged and my fellow angler applauded. I quickly measured the bass, by far my biggest ever. It was longer than my cooler was wide, which put it at 23 inches or more. I'm sure it would have

Billy Goat Becomes Just an Old Goat

One of the areas where I can manage to avoid a crowd of anglers, even during the height of steelhead mania, is a breakwall about 25 miles from where I live.

The west side of this harbor breakwall is a long concrete pier easily accessible to anglers and, consequently, very popular certain times of year. The east side, however, is a 300-yard stretch of massive jumbled boulders, many weighing several tons. Some are packed close together. Some require a leap to get from one boulder to another. I didn't fish it very often because traversing it was arduous and dangerous, especially when laden with all the gear carried by some poor fool suffering from Boy Scout Syndrome.

But every once in a while I'd venture out, at least partway, to find a small piece of Lake Ontario that I could call my own.

I did this one November day not many years ago. It was a bitterly cold day with a strong wind. No one else was there, and the emptiness beckoned me. I carefully maneuvered most of the first 100 yards without mishap and was only one jump from where I wanted to be. I was encumbered in my usual fashion: 20-pound bag over my right shoulder, thermos and net in my left hand, two rods (the second one "just in case") in my right.

I jumped and didn't quite make it. I teetered and began to fall backward into a 10-foot crevice between boulders. Instinctively, I shot my left hand down to break my fall. This I managed to do, but I felt a searing pain in my hand, elbow,

and shoulder from the impact. I'm still not sure how I regained my feet, but I did, shaking from the effort and relieved that I hadn't killed myself. If I'd tumbled to the bottom of that crevice and broken my leg or neck, it might have been days before I was found. If the fall didn't kill me, hypothermia would have. But I was OK. I'd even managed to hang onto my thermos and net while breaking my fall, though the steel thermos had a brand-new dent. And blood on it. Hmmm.

My hands were very cold, quite numb, but I could see that I had split the top of my left thumb about halfway down the nail on both sides. Looking at the new gap, with the blood welling up, made me nauseated. There was a small hospital in town, so I *very* carefully made my way back to my car. A lady who worked at the bait shop nearby kindly found me a couple Band-Aids and patched me up. (I knew I had some somewhere, but was too shaken and shocked to start digging through my stuff.)

By the time I got to the hospital my thumb was throbbing painfully and my arm and shoulder ached. Luckily, the emergency room wasn't busy, and they attended to me right away. The doctor gave me a few stitches and a painkiller, bandaged me, and managed not to tell me what an idiot I was. She was a nice doctor.

I counted my blessings while driving home that evening. And came to a realization: I was no longer the 17-year-old billy goat hopping easily from rock to rock and plucking fish from the rapids. I was a late forty-something old goat who needed to look, and think, twice before he leapt. ◄◄◄

tipped the scales at 6 pounds, beating my previous best by a good 2 pounds.

Despite the short fight, it took a little while for the bass to revive and escape my grasp. I knew then that he was an old warrior nearing the end of his days. He probably wouldn't see another summer. He was a magnificent fish, though, and I felt grateful and blessed to have made his acquaintance.

There was no way I was going to top that fish, so I went back to the cottage, drenched to the bone and deeply, profoundly content.

Evolution of an Angler and Why I Love to Fish

If you are over forty years of age, chances are your political views are not the same as they were when you were twenty.

If you are a parent, the ranking of important things in your life is radically different from when you were not.

My desire to become a good fisherman hasn't changed since I was a child. But my definition of a good fisherman sure has.

It's no longer about quantity or quality or even consistency. It's not about catching fish when others aren't or catching more when they are getting a few.

It's about respecting and appreciating fish, the environment, and the rights of other anglers while enjoying every aspect of every moment on the water.

I need to tread carefully here because I don't want to sermonize. I'm quick to bristle when someone attempts to foist their values or belief systems on me. So consider what follows as a rambling, personal statement of beliefs; a suit of clothes that I have grown into comfortably but that isn't necessarily "one size fits all."

I believe that anyone who spends a great deal of time in the outdoors learns an appreciation of, and respect for, nature. After all, it's only "natural." Fields, forests, and streams are more beautiful to most of us than concrete and steel.

At one time, humans were as inextricably a part of nature's web as bears, birds, or fish. We took shelter in caves, drank and washed in streams, hunted, fished, and foraged for what was available. We lived off the land we were part of, subject to nature's cruel whimsy, benefiting from her bounty.

"Normal" evolution takes tens of thousands, even millions, of years. Changes, while inexorable and cumulative, are also infinitesimal.

Until we came along.

In just a few thousand years—a teardrop in the ocean of time—we have transformed ourselves and our world.

Our buildings, the most visible sign of our rapid "evolution," were designed to be protective cocoons, shields against nature's extremes. Most of us live and work in these cocoons. We travel between the two in mobile cocoons.

For many of us, nature is what we experience from front door to front seat, from parking lot to lobby.

On nice days, some of us experience nature by eating lunch and strolling about in a park while admiring the manicured greenness of the grass and the symmetry of the flower gardens. The closest encounter many of us have with wildlife is feeding pigeons, visiting a zoo, or tuning into a *National Geographic* special.

Our cocoons have gone beyond their original purpose. They not only insulate, they isolate.

In times of war, dehumanizing the enemy has long been an established tactic. It is simply easier to kill someone if he is not truly one of "us."

Alienation is more subtle, but has a similar effect. Most of us don't spend a lot of time worrying about those on the fringes of society until we read a headline about some "loner" striking out. Then our response is to shake our heads and lock our doors. It's easier to hurt or ignore something if it doesn't feel like part of our everyday life.

Many, if not most of us, are leading lives alienated from nature.

We tend to only pay attention when Mother Nature throws a tantrum, when a hurricane, tornado, or earthquake makes it to the top of the news. If a big storm is headed our way, we reinforce our cocoons.

I'm not advising a stroll through the nearest tornado or recommending that you camp in a blizzard. And you certainly don't have to be an angler to appreciate the outdoors. But you *do* need a reason to be "out there" in all kinds of weather, whether it's hunting, camping, hiking, or bird-watching.

Fishing is my chosen umbilical chord, one that reconnects me with nature.

If not for fishing, I wouldn't have been so cold that I now never take warmth for granted. I would never go so many hours without eating that a hard-boiled egg (without salt!) tastes like haute cuisine.

If not for fishing, I wouldn't know the delicious sensation of soaking my hat in the water, putting it back on, and feeling the cooling drops dribble down my face and the nape of my neck after hours under a broiling sun.

If not for fishing, I wouldn't have been awed by hundred of dawns and dusks, painted with an infinitely varied palette. I wouldn't have watched moving curtains of rain sweep across a lake—sometimes missing me, most often not—occasionally followed by brilliant rainbows.

If not for fishing, I wouldn't know the meaning of absolute silence; the perfect stillness and quiet experienced while standing at the end of the dock in the predawn darkness. I only realize how mesmerizing the absence of sound can be when a loon's mournful cry fills the void, echoes for a lingering moment and then fades.

If not for fishing, I might have forgotten just how wonderful the feeling of anticipation is. The start of a day on the water is like Christmas Eve when I was six years old. And I can experience it much more often than once a year.

If not for fishing, I wouldn't know the groaning sound a dead tree makes when leaning against one of its brothers. I wouldn't have been enchanted by the endless, gurgling chatter of a set of rapids. I wouldn't have been nearly hypnotized by the swirl of an eddy.

If not for fishing, I would never have realized how comfortable I can be while alone. Conversely, I wouldn't have spent so many pleasant hours with friends and family, sharing the intimacy of a confined space by swapping lies, confiding problems, or just enjoying a companionable silence.

If not for fishing, I wouldn't have experienced the unique sensation of being perfectly relaxed, absolutely at ease one moment, and then, in the split second it takes for a line to twitch or a float to dip, becoming charged with adrenaline-fueled, pulse-pounding excitement.

And fishing has allowed me to experience these wonders *thousands* of times! How can I not be grateful? How can I not love it?

I have long been drawn to the animistic beliefs of many Aboriginal peoples. Common among many is the belief that spirits reside in all things, and they, or some of their qualities, can be invoked or absorbed by partaking in certain activities, eating certain foods, or dreaming special dreams.

I don't know if I've actually absorbed them, but I have certainly been moved by the raw power of a salmon or carp. I've thrilled a thousand times to the cartwheeling frenzy of a runaway rainbow. I've admired the suspicious bait-nosing of a wily brown and the dogged determination of a smallmouth. I've laughed at the more-guts-than-brains attacks of perch on lures twice their size. I have been struck dumb by the beauty of a speckled trout dressed in its best spawning colors.

And I consistently marvel at how seamlessly these creatures meld with their habitat. Fish are truly one with their world, the way we used to be.

Often, while sitting on a log or a rock, mentally adrift in that limbo between bites, I begin to fancy that I'm starting to belong there, that roots are about to spring from my boots and moss may start to form on my arms and legs. I feel I am becoming a part of where I am.

When I was a child I read a book that matter-of-factly stated that Native Americans could walk through the woods without making a sound. It said that early settlers feared them for their ghostly ability to appear and disappear silently. How marvelous that seemed!

I wanted to be like that. I tried to walk stealthily, but I would always snap a twig or crackle a dry leaf.

Fish *are* like that, ghostly and mysterious, there and then not there.

I am on my way to becoming the fisherman I want to be, but I'm not nearly there yet.

I will have achieved what I aspire to when I am no longer an interloper on the water. When I walk away from a muddy bank and leave no boot prints. When even a sharp-eyed osprey cannot distinguish me from the rock I am sitting on. When I can arrive, and ultimately leave, without snapping a twig or leaving a ripple.

A P P E N D I X

Primer—Equipment Basics for the Beginner

What follows is a brief overview of the three main fishing outfits used in freshwater angling (fly-fishing excepted). I've also included information on some of the terminal tackle referred to throughout the book ("terminal" means the end of, or near the end of, your line).

Spinning

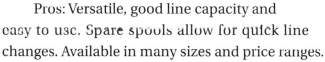

This is the type of open-faced spinning outfit I refer to throughout the book.

OPEN-FACE REEL WITH ROD

Pros: Versatile, good line capacity and easy to use. Spare spools allow for quick line changes. Available in many sizes and price ranges.

Cons: Not particularly well suited for traditional monofilament lines of large diameter (those over 20-pound test).

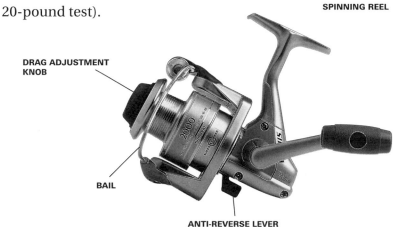

SPINNING REEL

DRAG ADJUSTMENT KNOB

BAIL

ANTI-REVERSE LEVER

SHIMANO (2)

153

Spincast

Many of us grew up using this outfit, and some of us never grew out of it.

Pros: Very easy to use. Most working parts are enclosed, keeping them relatively safe from young, curious fingers.

Cons: Limited line capacity, making them a poor choice for long-line trolling. Not much selection in the tackle shops, especially at the higher end of the quality scale, due to the popularity of spinning outfits.

SPINCASTER

Baitcasting

Level-wind casting outfits are favored by many largemouth bass and muskie anglers.

Pros: Very well suited for the new, thinner, ultrastrong "super" lines, making them a favorite for fishing heavy cover for bass or when pursuing big fish like muskie or pike. Very reliable drag system. Good selection available in price ranges from medium to very high.

Cons: Casting proficiency has a high learning curve, making them difficult to master. Not a good choice for casting very light lures or bait.

BAITCASTER

ABU GARCIA (2)

Sinkers

Sinkers are designed to help get your lure or bait down to where the fish are. They come in an enormous variety of shapes and sizes (weights), but

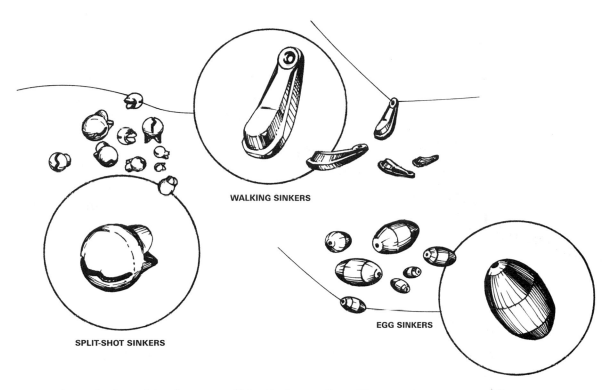

WALKING SINKERS

SPLIT-SHOT SINKERS

EGG SINKERS

most are designed to clamp or slide onto your line. The most common of the clamp-on types are round split shot, often with little "ears" that make them removable. Of the slide-ons, I most often use egg and walking sinkers.

Originally, sinkers were made exclusively of lead, but many jurisdictions have banned the use of this metal. Steel, tin, and bismuth are the most common substitutes.

Hooks

There are a multitude of hook styles and sizes. Only a few are shown here. Your local tackle shop is the perfect place to ogle the huge assortment.

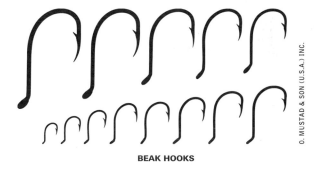

BEAK HOOKS

O. MUSTAD & SON (U.S.A.) INC.

The "beak" style of bait hook can be used to fish everything from tiny worms for trout to hunks of chicken liver for catfish.

The slightly longer shank of the Kirby hook makes hook removal a little easier, particularly when fishing for fish with small mouths, like sunfish and other panfish.

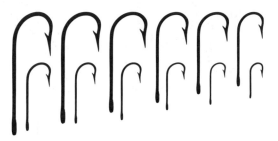

KIRBY HOOKS

O. MUSTAD & SON (U.S.A.) INC.

Other Terminal Tackle

Swivels, snap swivels, leaders, and split rings belong in every well-stocked vest or tackle box.

Swivels reduce line twist. Snap swivels are tied to the end of the line and then attached to some lures (see chapter 3, Lures).

Steel leaders are ideal if you're angling for "toothy" fish—fish that may bite through your standard monofilament line and make off with your expensive lure.

Split rings are attached to some lures, and then your line to the ring. They can also

THREE-WAY SWIVEL

BALL-BEARING BARREL SWIVEL

BALL-BEARING SWIVELS WITH COAST LOCK

BALL-BEARING SWIVEL

SPRO (4)

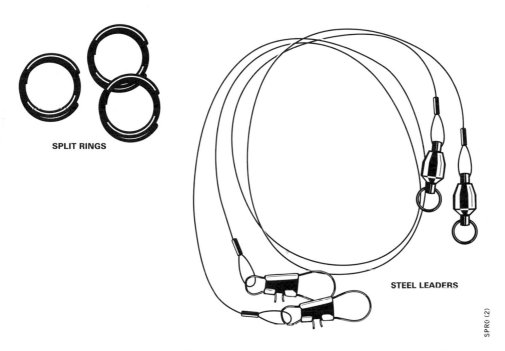

SPLIT RINGS

STEEL LEADERS

SPRO (2)

be used to replace damaged hooks on some lures. (Some lures use split rings to attach the hooks to the screw-eye imbedded in the lure body. If a hook breaks, it can easily be replaced with a new split ring and hook.)

INDEX

Numbers in **bold** refer to pages with illustrations.